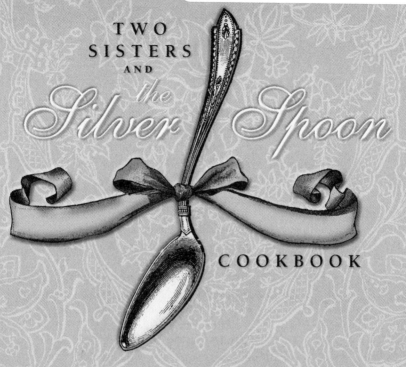

TWO
SISTERS
AND
the
Silver Spoon
COOKBOOK

"GUARANTEED
NOT TO TARNISH
YOUR IMAGE"

Some of the proceeds of
Two Sisters and The Silver Spoon
will be donated to the Melanoma Research Fund
to support the research of Dr. Michael B. Atkins of
Beth Israel Deaconess Medical Center,
Boston, Massachusetts.

To order additional copies of
Two Sisters and The Silver Spoon
send check or money order for
$26.95 each plus $5.00 shipping and handling
(*Massachusetts residents add 5% sales tax*) to:
Two Sisters and The Silver Spoon Cookbook
P.O. Box 4
Rochdale, MA 01542
email: info@twosisterscookbook.com
website: www.twosisterscookbook.com
(allow 2 to 3 weeks for delivery)

Photographer: Melikian Studio,
Worcester, Massachusetts

Set Design: Rose Seed

ISBN: 978-09815753-0-8

WIMMER
COOKBOOKS

A CONSOLIDATED GRAPHICS COMPANY

800.548.2537   wimmerco.com

Introduction

We are proud to say we are the daughters of two wonderful parents. As children, we had instilled in us the importance of family, hard work, love of country and giving to others.

Our father was a World War II veteran that fought in the European Theatre and the Battle of the Bulge. Today, we continue to support the veteran's groups that our father was affiliated with. Growing up, our mother was the traditional "stay at home Mom." She kept an immaculate house and had a passion for antiquing. Collecting antique dishes and fine English bone china teacups were two of the collections she adored most. What our parents were all about, lives on in the two of us.

As elementary school teachers, making a difference in children's lives has been our aspiration. We have tried to incorporate the things we love into our every day teaching.

We were inspired with the love of cooking at an early age. Our father was Armenian and our mother was Spanish. As a result, family recipes from these two cultures were in abundance. Throughout our travels within our great country, we have also incorporated delicious recipes from the regions we love into this cookbook.

We take pleasure in cooking and entertaining in a grand style incorporating antiques, beautiful linens and delicious menus. Between our family homes in central Massachusetts and our home on Cape Cod, we have enjoyed sharing our culinary talents and flare for entertaining in these two unique settings with family and friends.

Being sustaining members of the Junior League of Worcester in Worcester, Massachusetts and bell ringers for the Salvation Army are community services to which we are committed.

A very important cause of ours is to support Melanoma research. Our dear Mother passed away from melanoma. It is our desire to contribute some of the proceeds of this cookbook to the research and development of new ways in treating, prolonging the lives of its victims and ultimately finding a cure for this disease.

"*We make a living by what we get.*
We make a life by what we give."

~ SIR WINSTON CHURCHILL

Table of Contents

Notes

Appetizers & Beverages

"Glass, china and reputation are
easily cracked and never well mended."

~ Benjamin Franklin

Armenian Easter Eggs "Naturally"

1 dozen brown eggs   4 cups dry outer onion skins

Eggs can be colored with natural dyes. With this family recipe, take the dry onion skins and place in a large pot of water. Bring to boil. Reduce heat and simmer 30 minutes. Remove from heat and cool. May place pot in the refrigerator to speed up cooling. Gently place 6 eggs at a time into water with skins. Return to boil. Reduce heat and simmer 15 minutes. Repeat with remaining eggs. Turn eggs gently with a wooden spoon. The color will be ocher, a moderate to deep brownish orange.

Yield: Dozen colored eggs

The motion of the eggs in the boiling water ensures that the color will cover the entire egg. Our Mother traditionally made these on Holy Thursday, just as our paternal grandmother did. They are a family favorite. It would not be Easter without them.

Cocktail Whiskey Dogs

1½ cups ketchup   2 pounds skinless hotdogs, cut
½ cup packed dark brown sugar   1-inch thick
                                      ¾ cup whiskey

Combine ketchup, brown sugar and hot dogs in a saucepan. Bring to boil. Reduce heat and simmer 25 minutes. Add whiskey and simmer an additional 25 minutes.

Yield: 8 to 10 servings

We have been making this recipe for so many years. It is one of our favorites. They can be made in advance. Serve warm with toothpicks.

Easy Chicken Wings

½ cup soy sauce
¼ cup honey

¼ cup sugar
2 pounds chicken wings,
 rinsed and patted dry

Whisk together soy sauce, honey and sugar. Place wings in a large bowl. Pour sauce over wings and coat well. Marinate overnight. Cover and bake at 350 degrees 1 hour. Uncover and bake an additional 15 minutes.

Yield: 6 to 8 servings

Crab Cakes
"The Breakers" Style

1 tablespoon olive oil
1 teaspoon finely chopped onions
1 teaspoon finely chopped sweet red
 pepper
1 teaspoon finely chopped yellow
 pepper
1 teaspoon chopped green onions
¼ teaspoon "Kick On" spices
¼ cup bread crumbs

1 tablespoon mayonnaise
1 dash Tabasco sauce
1 dash lemon juice
1 dash Worcestershire sauce
1 cup jumbo lump crabmeat
Salt and pepper to taste
¼ cup vegetable oil
¼ cup all-purpose flour

Heat oil in a heavy skillet. Sauté onions, red pepper, yellow pepper and green onions until tender. Cool in the refrigerator. Combine vegetables with spice, bread crumbs, mayonnaise, Tabasco, juice, Worcestershire sauce, crabmeat, salt and pepper. Shape mixture into 12 small patties. Heat oil in a skillet. Dust patties in flour. Sauté on both sides until golden browned. Transfer to a buttered baking sheet. Bake at 350 degrees 15 minutes or until center is hot.

Yield: 12 crab cakes

Cape Cod Lobster Cakes

"KICK ON" SPICES

2½ tablespoons paprika
2 tablespoons onion salt
2 tablespoons garlic powder
2½ teaspoons pepper
1 tablespoon cayenne pepper

1 tablespoon dried oregano
1 tablespoon dried thyme
½ teaspoon dried lemon peel
½ teaspoon ground chipotle pepper
(optional)

Combine paprika, onion salt, garlic powder, pepper, cayenne, oregano, thyme, lemon peel and chipotle pepper. Store spice in a small jar. It may be used in marinades and as a seasoning for chicken, fish, pork or beef.

TARTAR SAUCE

¾ cup mayonnaise
2 tablespoons chopped green
onions, green part only

2 tablespoons sweet pickle relish,
drained
1 tablespoon capers, drained
1 tablespoon lemon juice

Combine mayonnaise, onions, relish, capers and juice. Mix well. Refrigerate until ready to serve lobster cakes.

LOBSTER CAKES

1 cup finely chopped onions
½ cup finely chopped celery
¼ cup chopped sweet red pepper
¼ cup chopped yellow pepper
2 tablespoons unsalted butter
Salt and cayenne pepper to taste
1 tablespoon chopped garlic
1 pound lobster meat, diced
¼ cup green onions, green part only
½ cup mayonnaise

1 teaspoon lemon juice
2 tablespoons finely chopped
parsley
1 tablespoon Creole mustard
¼ cup all-purpose flour
2 teaspoons "Kick On" spice
1 large egg
1½ cups fine dry bread crumbs
1 cup vegetable oil

(continued on next page)

(Cape Cod Lobster Cakes continued)

Sauté onions, celery and peppers in butter. Add salt and cayenne. Cook and stir 5 minutes until slightly golden browned. Add garlic and cook 2 minutes. Cool 5 minutes. Combine lobster, onions, mayonnaise, juice, parsley, mustard, ¾ cup bread crumbs and cooked vegetables in a large bowl. Mix well. Shape mixture into 10 patties.

In a shallow bowl, combine flour and 1 teaspoon "Kick On" spice. In a second bowl, whisk together egg with small amount of water. In a third bowl, combine ¾ cup bread crumbs and remaining 1 teaspoon "Kick On" spice. Heat oil in a large skillet over medium high heat. Dredge patties in flour mixture. Tap off excess. Dip in egg wash, letting excess drip off. Gently place patties in bread crumb mixture. Shake off excess. Fry until lightly golden browned.

Yield: 10 cakes

These lobster cakes are a delightful start to any meal or may be enjoyed at a luncheon. A wonderful compliment to this special dish would be a nice glass of champagne.

Summer Bruschetta

3 large ripe tomatoes, seeded and
  chopped
½ large red onion, diced
1 cucumber, peeled, seeded and
  diced
1 cup basil leaves, shredded

Salt and pepper to taste
¼ cup extra-virgin olive oil
1 tablespoon red wine vinegar
1 loaf Italian peasant bread
3 garlic cloves, peeled

Combine tomatoes, onions, cucumber, basil, salt and pepper. Add oil and vinegar and toss well. Let stand at room temperature 1 hour. Cut bread into ½-inch thick slices. Cut slices in half diagonally. Lightly brush one side with oil. Grill or broil until toasted. Rub hot bread with garlic on oiled side. Sprinkle with salt and pepper. Top with vegetable mixture.

Yield: 15 to 20 servings

Skewered Chicken

1½ pounds boneless, skinless
  chicken breast halves, cut into
  ¾-inch cubes
1 tablespoon balsamic vinegar
⅓ cup red wine
½ cup chutney
¼ cup olive oil

1 bell pepper, seeded and cut
  into 1-inch squares
1 sweet red pepper, seeded and
  cut into 1-inch squares
1 yellow pepper, seeded and cut
  into 1-inch squares

Combine chicken, vinegar, red wine, chutney and oil. Stir to coat. Marinate overnight. Drain chicken. Thread 2 chicken pieces on skewers, alternating with 2 peppers. Grill over hot coals 8 to 10 minutes.

Yield: 6 servings

Skewered Tortellini

1 cup Crème Fraîche
¼ cup Parmesan cheese
Zest of 2 lemons
Juice of 2 lemons

3 roasted garlic cloves, peeled
  and crushed
1½ pounds tortellini, mixed colors
Olive oil
40 wooden skewers

Combine Crème Fraîche, Parmesan cheese, zest, juice and garlic. Refrigerate Parmesan Lemon Dip until ready to use. Bring lightly salted water to boil in a large pan. Add tortellini and cook until tender. Drain pasta and toss with oil. Skewer two tortellini on each stick. Serve with Parmesan Lemon Dip.

Yield: 20 servings

Caramel Butter Brie

1 stick butter
½ cup packed brown sugar
½ cup sugar
½ cup heavy cream

¼ teaspoon ground nutmeg
1 (12-ounce) wheel Brie cheese
⅛ cup sliced and toasted
   almonds

Melt butter, brown sugar and sugar in a saucepan until sugars are dissolved. Gradually add cream, beating until smooth. Stir in nutmeg. Cook until thickened and caramelized. Place Brie in a pie plate. Pour caramel sauce over top. Bake at 225 degrees 10 minutes or until Brie softens to desired consistency. Remove from oven and sprinkle with almonds. Let stand 5 minutes before serving.

Yield: 8 servings

Herbed Mozzarella Appetizer

¾ pound fresh mozzarella cheese
½ cup extra-virgin olive oil
2 tablespoons chopped mixed basil
   and parsley
1 garlic clove, minced
¼ teaspoon crushed red pepper
¼ teaspoon salt

¼ teaspoon pepper
1 (2-ounce) jar oil-cured olives
1 (7-ounce) jar sun-dried tomatoes,
   drained
1 (7-ounce) jar roasted red peppers,
   cut into strips
1 loaf French bread

Drain cheese and cut into ½-inch cubes. Combine cheese, oil, herbs, garlic, red pepper, salt and pepper. Toss gently to coat. Cover and refrigerate at least 12 hours, stirring occasionally. To serve, let cheese return to room temperature. Using a slotted spoon, mound cheese in the center of a serving platter. Arrange olives, tomatoes and peppers around cheese. Serve with crusty French bread or cocktail forks.

Yield: 8 servings

Gorgonzola Cheese Spread

1 (8-ounce) package cream cheese, softened
5 ounces Gorgonzola cheese, crumbled
¼ cup chopped black olives
¼ teaspoon black pepper
Dash of garlic powder
½ cup diced roasted red peppers
Crackers or vegetable crudités

Combine cream cheese and Gorgonzola cheese in a blender. Pulse until blended. Add olives, pepper, garlic powder and peppers. Pulse until well combined. Refrigerate until ready to serve. Serve with crackers or vegetable crudités.

Yield: 6 to 8 servings

Valentine Cherry Cheese Spread

1 (8-ounce) package cream cheese, cubed
4 ounces Havarti cheese, cubed
1 cup shredded smoky Swiss cheese
¼ cup crumbled blue cheese
¼ cup slivered almonds
3 tablespoons cherry flavored liqueur
1 teaspoon chopped shallot
¼ cup dried cherries, chopped
Cheesecloth
French bread, assorted crackers or celery sticks

Allow all cheeses stand at room temperature for at least 30 minutes to soften. Line a heart shaped mold with cheesecloth. Spread almonds on an ungreased baking sheet. Bake at 350 degrees 5 to 7 minutes or until golden browned, stirring occasionally. Cool. Combine all cheeses, liqueur and shallot in a food processor. Process until smooth. Add cherries and almonds. Process with on/off pulses until almonds are chopped. Spread cheese mixture into mold. Cover and refrigerate at least 24 hours to blend flavors. About 30 minutes before serving, unmold cheese onto plate. Remove cheesecloth. Let stand room temperature to soften. Serve with thin slices baguette style French bread, crackers or celery sticks.

Yield: 2¼ cups

Maple Sweetened Goat Cheese

1 (3-ounce) mild goat cheese
⅓ cup toasted walnuts
1 ripe Bosc pear, sliced

4 teaspoons maple syrup
Assorted crackers

Place cheese in the center of an antique serving plate. Arrange nuts and pear slices around cheese. Pour syrup over cheese and serve immediately with crackers and a glass of vintage port.

Yield: 4 servings

Southern Pecan Baked Brie

1 whole small Brie cheese wheel
1 cup crushed pecans

1 cup packed brown sugar

Slice top and sides off cheese. Mound pecans over cheese. Sprinkle brown sugar over pecans. Bake at 350 degrees 20 to 25 minutes or until bubbly.

Yield: 4 to 6 servings

Sun-Dried Tomato and Brie

½ (7-ounce) jar sun-dried
    tomatoes, packed in oil
1 shallot
¼ onion

Basil to taste
1 medium Brie cheese wheel
Bagel chips or crackers

Blend tomatoes, shallot, onion and basil in food processor. Remove top wax layer of Brie. Spread tomato mixture on top. Microwave 30 seconds. Brie should be soft not runny. Serve with bagel chips or crackers.

Yield: 6 to 8 servings

Pineapple Cheese Ball

2 (8-ounce) packages cream cheese, softened
1 (7-ounce) can pineapple, well drained
2 tablespoons finely chopped onion
¼ cup chopped celery

1 cup chopped pecans
1 (4-ounce) can chopped green chilies, minced
Dash of seasoned salt
Assorted crackers or celery

Blend cream cheese, pineapple, onions, celery, pecans, chilies and salt. Roll mixture into a ball and refrigerate overnight. May roll ball in additional chopped pecans. Serve with crackers or spread on celery.

Yield: 6 to 8 servings

Holiday Cheese Balls

1 (8-ounce) package cream cheese, softened
1 (4-ounce) package blue cheese, softened
1 tablespoon Tabasco sauce
1 tablespoon Tabasco green pepper sauce

1 garlic clove, minced
2 (8-ounce) packages shredded sharp Cheddar cheese
⅔ cup dried cranberries
½ cup finely chopped walnuts
½ cup finely chopped parsley

Combine cream cheese, blue cheese, Tabasco sauces and garlic in a food processor. Process until well blended. Add Cheddar cheese and cranberries and blend well. Shape mixture into two balls and wrap in wax paper. Refrigerate several hours. Combine walnuts and parsley. Roll balls in nut mixture. Wrap in plastic wrap until ready to serve.

Yield: 2 cheese balls

Cream Cheese Filled Strawberries

1 (8-ounce) package cream
   cheese, softened
2 tablespoons sugar
1 tablespoon vanilla

16 large strawberries, trimmed
   and cored
Slivered almonds and fresh mint
   leaves for garnish

Beat cream cheese, sugar and vanilla until smooth. Spoon mixture into a pastry bag fitted with a star tip. Pipe filling into strawberries. Garnish with almond slivers and mint.

Yield: 4 to 6 servings

Especially delightful during the strawberry season!

Holiday Pinecone Spread

1¼ cups whole almonds
1 (8-ounce) package cream cheese,
   softened
½ cup mayonnaise
5 slices bacon, cooked crisp and
   crumbled

1 tablespoon chopped
   green onions
½ teaspoon dried dill
⅛ teaspoon pepper
Assorted crackers

Spread almonds in a single layer on a baking sheet. Bake at 300 degrees 15 minutes, stirring often until almonds turn color. Blend cream cheese and mayonnaise. Add bacon, onions, dill and pepper. Mix well. Cover and refrigerate overnight. Form mixture into shapes of two pinecones on a serving platter. Beginning at top narrow end, press almonds in at a slight angle into cheese mixture in rows. Continue overlapping rows until all cheese is covered. Cover the ends of real pine sprigs with plastic wrap and garnish top of cheese pinecones. Serve with crackers.

Yield: 6 to 8 servings

Snow Peas with Boursin

50 to 60 tender young snow peas   Fresh mint leaves (optional)
8 ounces Boursin cheese, softened

Remove stem end from snow peas and string peas. Blanch peas in boiling water 30 seconds. Plunge into cool water to stop cooking. Using a small sharp knife, slit open the straight seam of each snow pea. Spoon cheese into a small tipped pastry bag. Pipe cheese into each snow pea. Garnish with mint.

Yield: 10 to 12 servings

For the holidays, the pea pods may be placed on a silver platter in the shape of a Christmas tree or wreath. Instead of the mint, garnish each with a tiny piece of pimento.

Cucumber Boats

4 seedless English cucumbers   ½ teaspoon salt
4 tablespoons extra-virgin olive oil   ¼ teaspoon pepper
2 teaspoons sherry vinegar   2 tablespoons coarsely chopped
1 cup crumbled feta cheese   fresh oregano

Slice cucumbers lengthwise and scoop out any seeds making a well. Take two cucumber halves and cut into ¼-inch diced pieces. Transfer to a bowl. Add oil, vinegar, cheese, salt and pepper. Toss well. Add oregano and toss again. To the remaining six cucumber halves, remove one or two long strips from the underside with a vegetable peeler. The cucumbers will sit without tipping. Divide the cheese mixture among boats. Slice cucumbers on a slight diagonal into 1½-inch sections. Serve immediately.

Yield: 18 to 20 servings

We have served these at our Memorial Day parties on Cape Cod. Everyone loved these cucumber boats.

Citrus Fruit Cocktail

3 oranges
1 grapefruit

2 tablespoons powdered sugar
Mint leaves for garnish (optional)

Peel and segment fruit. Discard membranes. Add sugar and mix well. Refrigerate. Serve in ice cold cocktail glasses. Garnish with mint.

Yield: 4 servings

Roquefort Cheese Grapes

1 (10-ounce) package pecans,
   almonds or walnuts
1 (8-ounce) package cream cheese,
   softened

½ cup Roquefort cheese
2 tablespoons heavy cream
1 pound seedless red or green
   grapes, rinsed and dried

Spread nuts in a single layer on a baking sheet. Bake at 275 degrees until toasted. Pecans and walnuts will smell toasted. Do not burn. Almonds will be golden browned. Place nuts in a food processor. Chop coarsely and spread on a plate. Beat cream cheese, Roquefort cheese and cream until smooth. Add grapes and gently stir by hand to coat grapes. Roll grapes in nuts. Place on a wax paper lined baking sheet. Refrigerate until ready to serve.

Yield: about 50 hors d'oeuvres

For a decorative touch, arrange to form grape cluster.

Bourbon Blue Cheese

1 (8-ounce) package cream cheese, softened
1 (4-ounce) container Maytag Blue cheese, softened
5 tablespoons butter, softened
1 garlic clove, crushed
Dash of Tabasco sauce
Dash of Worcestershire sauce
¼ teaspoon salt
¼ teaspoon pepper
3 tablespoons Kentucky bourbon
Assorted crackers or sesame sticks

Beat cream cheese, blue cheese and butter until smooth. Add garlic, Tabasco, Worcestershire sauce, salt, pepper and bourbon. Mix well. Cover and refrigerate at least 24 hours. Serve with crackers or sesame sticks.

Yield: 8 to 10 servings

Eggplant Caponata

2 medium eggplants, cubed
1 small bell pepper, chopped
1 medium onion, chopped
¾ cup sliced mushrooms
2 garlic cloves, crushed
⅓ cup vegetable oil
1 (6-ounce) can tomato paste
¼ cup water
2 tablespoons wine vinegar
½ cup Spanish olives, sliced
1½ teaspoons sugar
½ teaspoon dried oregano
1 teaspoon salt
⅛ teaspoon pepper
French or Syrian bread, sliced

Sauté eggplant, peppers, onions, mushrooms, garlic in oil until tender. Add tomato paste, water, vinegar, olives, sugar, oregano, salt and pepper. Cook and stir 30 minutes. Refrigerate overnight. Serve cold with French bread or Syrian bread.

Yield: 15 to 20 servings

May serve warm over pasta or a side dish with chicken.

Orange Glazed Melon Balls

1 ripe cantaloupe
1 ripe honey dew melon

⅓ cup Mandarin Napoleon brandy
⅓ cup fresh mint leaves, chopped

Cut both melons in half. Scoop out seeds. With a melon ball scoop, cut out melon balls. Combine melon balls and brandy. Refrigerate until ready to serve. Prior to serving, sprinkle with mint.

Yield: 15 servings

This is pretty when served in an antique cut glass bowl.

Stuffed Dates

1 (16-ounce) package pitted dates
1 (4-ounce) package whole almonds

1¼ pounds bacon

Stuff each date with an almond. Cut bacon strips into thirds. Wrap each date with a bacon strip. Secure with a toothpick. Line a baking sheet with foil. Bake at 400 degrees 15 minutes or until bacon is crisp. Drain on a wire rack or paper towel. Serve warm.

Yield: about 60 hors d'oeuvres

Cranberry Pecan Spread

4 ounces cream cheese, softened
¼ cup chopped pecans

¼ cup dried cranberries
⅛ cup orange juice concentrate

Beat cream cheese until soft and fluffy. Add pecans, cranberries and juice. Mix well. Cover and refrigerate at least 30 minutes prior to serving.

Yield: 1 cup

A holiday spread that is quick and easy!

Baba Ghanouj

1 large eggplant
1 garlic clove, minced
3 tablespoons tahini
Juice of 1 lemon

Salt to taste
Chopped parsley for garnish
Pita bread, cut into wedges

Broil eggplant with skin on, turning on all sides. Cool slightly. Remove pulp and mash. Add garlic, tahini, juice and salt. Mix well. Garnish with parsley. Serve with pita wedges.

Yield: 6 servings

Colorful Vegetables with Dip

1 cup mayonnaise
1 teaspoon finely minced onion
1 tablespoon curry powder
3 tablespoons ketchup
1 tablespoon Worcestershire sauce
¼ teaspoon pepper

¼ teaspoon salt
Vegetables of choice, cut into pieces:
   celery, carrots, cauliflower,
   broccoli, cherry tomatoes,
   zucchini strips, sweet red bell
   pepper slices, green beans or
   strips of summer squash.

Combine mayonnaise, onions, curry, ketchup, Worcestershire sauce, pepper and salt. Mix well. Transfer to a round bowl and refrigerate. To serve, place bowl on a tray surrounded by cut vegetables.

Yield: 20 servings

May blanch carrots, broccoli, green beans and cauliflower to enhance their color.

Spicy Nut Honey with Blue Cheese

¼ cup walnuts
½ cup honey
¾ teaspoon cayenne pepper

4 ounces soft blue cheese
Sliced crusty bread or crackers

Toast walnuts at 350 degrees 10 to 12 minutes. Cool slightly and coarsely chop. Combine nuts, honey and cayenne. Spread small amount of cheese on bread slices and top with honey mixture.

Yield: 4 servings

May substitute goat cheese for blue cheese and ¼ teaspoon ground chipotle pepper for cayenne.

Charleston Cheese Spread

3½ cups shredded Cheddar cheese
1 cup mayonnaise
¼ teaspoon cayenne pepper
1 tablespoon minced onion
1 (8-ounce) can sliced water
  chestnuts, drained and coarsely
  chopped

¼ cup chopped, drained sun-dried
  tomatoes, in oil
1 tablespoon Worcestershire sauce
Assorted crackers

Combine cheese, mayonnaise, cayenne, onions, chestnuts, tomatoes and Worcestershire sauce. Mix well. Pour mixture into a 1-quart baking dish. Bake at 350 degrees 20 to 30 minutes or until bubbly. Serve with crackers.

Yield: 16 servings

Hummus

1 (15-ounce) can chickpeas
  (garbanzo beans)
3 tablespoons tahini
1 garlic clove, crushed

½ teaspoon salt
Juice of 1 lemon
½ cup water

Rinse peas in water until clear. Using a food processor, blend peas until smooth. Add tahini, garlic, salt, juice and water. Process until smooth.

Yield: 6 servings

Daffodil Dip

½ cup mayonnaise
1 (8-ounce) package cream cheese,
  softened
2 hard-cooked eggs, finely chopped
2 tablespoons chopped onions

⅛ teaspoon garlic powder
¼ teaspoon salt
⅛ teaspoon pepper
Parsley for garnish
Bread sticks or crackers

Blend mayonnaise and cream cheese. Add eggs, onions, garlic powder, salt and pepper. Mix well. Sprinkle with parsley. Serve with bread sticks or crackers.

Yield: 6 to 8 servings

In the spring, when daffodils bloom, celebrate by having a Daffodil Party! This dip is sure to be a hit!

"Winter's done, and April's in the skies;
Earth, look up with laughter in your eyes."

~ JOHN MANSFIELD

Cranberry Salsa with Brie

1½ cups cranberries
⅓ cup sugar
2 green onions, chopped
¼ cup chopped mint or cilantro
Zest of 1 lime
Juice of 1 lime

1 jalapeño pepper, seeded
  and minced
⅛ teaspoon salt
1 wheel Brie cheese
Assorted crackers

Combine cranberries, sugar, green onions, mint, zest, juice, pepper and salt in a food processor. Pulse on/off until mixture is coarsely chopped and has texture. Cover and refrigerate up to 8 hours. Pour salsa over room temperature Brie. Serve with crackers.

Yield: 12 to 15 servings

This salsa is wonderful at Thanksgiving and Christmas. It was a big hit when it was brought to Fogg's Farm for Thanksgiving dinner. Use as a condiment to turkey, pork or chicken.

Cucumber Dill Dip

1 (8-ounce) package cream cheese,
  softened
1 cup mayonnaise
2 medium cucumbers, peeled,
  seeded and chopped
2 tablespoons sliced green onions

1 tablespoon lemon juice
2 teaspoons snipped dill or
  ½ teaspoon dried
½ teaspoon Tabasco sauce
Assorted crackers

Beat cream cheese until smooth. Add mayonnaise, cucumbers, onions, juice, dill and Tabasco. Mix well. Cover and refrigerate. Serve with crackers.

Yield: 2½ cups

Mexican Caviar

2 (4¼-ounce) cans chopped ripe
    olives
2 (4-ounce) cans chopped green
    chilies
2 tomatoes, chopped
3 green onions, chopped
2 garlic cloves, crushed

1 tablespoon olive oil
2 teaspoons red wine vinegar
1 teaspoon pepper
¼ teaspoon salt
Tortilla chips

Combine olives, chiles, tomatoes, onions, garlic, oil, vinegar, pepper and salt.
Mix well. Cover and refrigerate overnight. Serve with tortilla chips.

Yield: 8 to 10 servings

*Plan on making this recipe when tomatoes are in season. Also makes a great
topping for pizza. May double the recipe and spread any leftover on top of a
frittata.*

Vidalia Onion Dip

1 cup chopped Vidalia onions
1 cup mayonnaise

1 cup shredded Cheddar cheese
Toast triangles or crackers

Combine onions, mayonnaise and cheese. Mix well. Pour mixture into a buttered
1½-quart baking dish. Bake at 350 degrees 20 minutes or until bubbly. Serve
with toast triangles or crackers.

Yield: 8 to 10 servings

*Vidalia onions are only available in spring and early summer. Should you choose
to substitute with another variety, make sure they are sweet onions.*

Strawberry Salsa

2 cups strawberries, rinsed,
   hulled and diced
¼ cup diced red onion
½ cup diced bell pepper
1 teaspoon salt
¼ teaspoon pepper

2 teaspoons minced cilantro or
   basil or 1 teaspoon dried
¼ teaspoon cayenne pepper
1 tablespoon vegetable oil
2 tablespoons honey
1 tablespoon lemon juice
Assorted crackers

Combine strawberries, onions, peppers, salt, pepper, cilantro, cayenne, oil, honey and juice. Mix well. Cover and refrigerate at least 2 hours. Serve with crackers.

Yield: 6 to 8 servings

May serve with grilled chicken. A delicious recipe when strawberries are in season!

Watermelon Salsa

¼ cup lime juice
2 tablespoons packed brown sugar
3 cups chopped seeded watermelon
1 cup chopped, seeded honeydew
   melon or cantaloupe
1 medium cucumber, peeled, seeded
   and chopped

½ cup chopped red onion
¼ cup chopped fresh mint
2 tablespoons finely chopped
   crystallized ginger
2 tablespoons minced seeded
   jalapeño chilies
Salt and pepper to taste

Whisk juice and sugar until sugar dissolves. Add watermelon, honeydew, cucumbers, onions, mint, ginger and jalapeños. Toss gently. Add salt and pepper. Cover and refrigerate up to 2 hours.

Yield: 4 cups

White Bean, Garlic and Tomato Salsa

1 garlic head
1 cup small white navy beans,
    drained and rinsed
3 medium tomatoes
1 small sweet onion, finely chopped

½ cup finely chopped basil leaves
2 tablespoons lemon juice
Salt and pepper to taste
Tortilla chips

Separate garlic into cloves. Discard loose papery outer skin, keeping inner skin intact. Wrap in foil, sealing seams tightly. Roast garlic at 400 degrees 30 minutes or until soft. Cool slightly. Peel off skin and mash garlic until smooth. Stir in beans. Dice two tomatoes and add to garlic. Quarter remaining tomato and purée until smooth in a food processor. Add to bean mixture. Stir in onions, basil and juice. Add salt and pepper and mix well. Cover and refrigerate at least 1 hour. Serve with tortilla chips.

Yield: 4 cups

*"Go confidently in the direction of your dreams.
Live the life you have imagined."*
~ Henry David Thoreau

Java Gold

10 whole cloves
2 cinnamon sticks, broken in half
¾ cup ground coffee,
   (decaffeinated optional)

¼ cup sugar
10 cups cold water
½ cup heavy cream, whipped
Cinnamon for garnish

Place cloves, cinnamon sticks and coffee in basket of automatic drip coffee maker. Place sugar in carafe of coffee maker. Brew coffee with cold water. Serve hot and top with cream and dust with cinnamon.

Yield: 10 cups

"Java Gold" won the Travers and Whitney Stakes in 1987.

Teddy Roosevelt's Libelous Mint Julep

Fresh mint leaves
1 sugar cube
½ cup rye whiskey
½ tablespoon brandy

Crushed ice
Sliced pineapple, banana and
   oranges
Maraschino cherries

Gently crush a few mint leaves with sugar and a good splash of water in the bottom of a silver Julep cup. Add whiskey and brandy. Fill the cup to the rim with crushed ice. Stir until the outside of the glass is thick with frost. Top with mint, pineapple, banana and orange slices and cherries.

Yield: 1 serving

"Key To The Mint" Julep

1 cup sugar
½ cup boiling water
Mint leaves

Crushed ice
100 proof Kentucky bourbon

Stir sugar in boiling water until sugar dissolves. Store simple syrup in a glass jar until ready to use. Place 3 to 4 mint leaves in a Julep glass. Add ice. Press down with spoon to bruise leaves. Add one ounce bourbon and one-half ounce syrup. Stir well. Pack glass with ice and fill with bourbon. Garnish with mint leaves.

Yield: 1 serving

Traditionally, this drink should be served in a silver julep cup on the first Saturday in May, during the most famous two minutes in sports history. "Key to the Mint" was named horse of the year in 1972.

Antipasti Martini

3 sprigs fresh rosemary
1 fennel stalk with leaves
6 sun-dried tomatoes, not packed
  in oil
2 garlic cloves
8 black Italian olives, oil cured

1 small yellow pepper, cut into
  strips
1 dry hot Italian pepper
1 small sweet red pepper, cut into
  strips
2 quarts top shelf vodka

Place rosemary, fennel, tomatoes, garlic, olives and all peppers in a decorative bottle. Pour in vodka and infuse for at least one day. Use spicy vodka to make your favorite Martini. Also gives Bloody Marys a real kick.

Yield: 2 quarts spicy vodka

Christmas Martini

6 parts vodka
1 part dry vermouth

1 teaspoon peppermint schnapps
Miniature candy cane

Combine vodka, vermouth and schnapps in a cocktail shaker with cracked ice. Shake well. Strain into a chilled martini glass. Garnish with candy cane.

Yield: 1 serving

Churchill's Martini

6 parts gin
Bottle of dry vermouth

Cocktail olives

Shake gin in a cocktail shaker with cracked ice. Strain into a chilled martini glass. Look at the bottle of vermouth! Garnish with olive.

Yield: 1 serving

Winston Churchill was a martini aficionado. Here is his recipe for a dry martini! Some people whisper "vermouth." Others, like Churchill, look at the bottle.

Listerine Martini

6 parts vodka
1 part blue curacao

Lemon twist

Combine vodka and curacao in a cocktail shaker with ice cubes. Shake well. Strain into a chilled martini glass. Garnish with a lemon twist.

Yield: 1 serving

This martini should be the color of Listerine's "Cool Mint." The original Listerine was formulated by Kathy's husband's great grandfather, Jordan Wheat Lambert.

Midnight in Palm Beach

3 parts raspberry flavored vodka   1 part sour mix
2 parts Chambord   Fresh raspberries and blackberries

Combine vodka, Chambord and sour mix in a cocktail shaker with cracked ice. Shake well. Strain into a chilled martini glass. Alternate raspberries and blackberries on a cocktail skewer. Place in glass.

Yield: 1 serving

A special drink, a special place.

Sea Island Peach Martini

6 parts vodka   Slice of peach
1 part peach schnapps

Combine vodka and schnapps in a cocktail shaker with cracked ice. Shake well. Strain into a chilled martini glass. Garnish with peach slice.

Yield: 1 serving

Valentine Martini

3 parts vodka   1 part Frangelico
3 parts chocolate liqueur   Chocolate curls

Combine vodka, chocolate liqueur and Frangelico in a cocktail shaker with ice cubes. Shake well. Strain into a chilled martini glass. Garnish with chocolate curls.

Yield: 1 serving

Bougainvillea

⅓ cup champagne   ⅓ cup cranberry juice
⅓ cup orange juice

Mix champagne, orange and cranberry juice. Pour over ice and serve.

Yield: 2 servings

Coronado Strawberry Lemonade

1 cup strawberries, hulled   2 (6-ounce) cans frozen lemonade
¼ cup sugar

Purée strawberries with sugar in a food processor. Prepare lemonade according to directions. Blend strawberries and lemonade.

Yield: 6 servings

Florida Sunset

1 (12-ounce) can frozen orange   3 cups water
    juice concentrate, thawed and   1 (750 milliliter) bottle champagne,
    undiluted   chilled or non-alcoholic
1 (12-ounce) can apricot nectar,   (optional)
    chilled   3 cups crushed ice
1½ pints strawberry sorbet,   Whole strawberries for garnish
    softened

Combine orange juice, apricot nectar, sorbet and water in a large container. Stir until blended. Refrigerate. To serve, pour mixture into a punch bowl. Add champagne and ice. Serve in stemmed glasses and garnish with strawberry.

Yield: 1 gallon

Peach Bellini

1 peach, peeled and pitted
Champagne

Edible flower for garnish

Purée peach and spoon into a glass. Add champagne. Garnish with flower.

Yield: 1 serving

Pink Sensation

¾ cup pink grapefruit juice cocktail   ½ cup raspberry sorbet

Place grapefruit juice and sorbet in a blender. Blend on high speed few seconds or until combined. Pour into a glass.

Yield: 1 serving

In case you did not know, we love pink!

Poinsettia

Pomegranate seeds
1 (46-ounce) bottle pomegranate
    juice

1 liter seltzer water

Place ¼ teaspoon seeds into each cube of ice cube tray. Fill with water and freeze. Fill antique stemmed crystal glasses with pomegranate ice cubes. Pour in juice to half full. Top with seltzer.

Yield: 8 to 12 servings

May substitute pomegranate juice with cranberry juice.

Rhubarb Iced Tea

8 stalks rhubarb, cut into 3-inch
   lengths
8 cups water

⅓ cup sugar or to taste
Fresh mint springs

Combine rhubarb and water in a large saucepan. Bring to boil. Reduce and simmer 1 hour. Strain liquid. To liquid, add sugar and stir until dissolved. Cool. Serve over ice in tall ice tea glasses. Garnish with mint sprig.

Yield: 4 servings

Here is another delicious drink that is "pink."

Spanish Sangría

1 (24-ounce) bottle dry red wine
2 tablespoons orange juice
2 tablespoons Grand Marnier™
1 tablespoon sugar

Orange and lemon slices
Peach wedges
1 cup club soda

Combine wine, juice, Grand Marnier™, sugar, orange slices, lemon slices and peach wedges in a large pitcher. Cover and refrigerate overnight. Add club soda and ice cubes. Serve very cold in balloon shaped wine glasses.

Yield: 4 cups

For Sangría Blanca, substitute 1 bottle dry white wine for red wine.

Strawberry Sparkle

¾ cup mashed strawberries   1 cup whole strawberries
1 (750 milliliter) bottle champagne
    or sparkling wine

Place mashed strawberries in the bottom of glass pitcher. Pour champagne into pitcher. Float in whole strawberries. Pour into chilled champagne flutes. Serve immediately.

Yield: 4 to 6 servings

Soups & Salads

"One must always wear a hat when lunching with people whom one does not know well. One appears to one's best advantage."

~ Coco Chanel

Chatham Lobster and Corn Chowder

6 tablespoons unsalted butter
½ cup finely chopped celery
1 medium onion, finely chopped
1 sweet red pepper, seeded and
  diced
2 tablespoons all-purpose flour
1 cup half-and-half

1 cup heavy cream
1 cup whole milk
¼ cup sherry
1 cup frozen white corn
1½-2 cups lobster meat, diced
Salt and white pepper to taste

Melt butter in a large stockpot. Sauté celery, onions and red pepper until tender. Sprinkle flour over vegetables and stir to coat. Add half-and-half, cream and milk. Stir gently until mixture boils and begins to thicken. Add sherry, corn and lobster meat. Reduce heat and heat thoroughly. Season with salt and pepper.

Yield: 4 servings

During late summer and into autumn, frozen corn may be substituted with 2 to 3 ears of fresh corn that has been steamed and removed from the cob. This is a favorite as a prelude to our Thanksgiving dinner.

Scallop Soup

2 cups milk
1 cup heavy cream
2 tablespoons butter
1 teaspoon salt
¼ teaspoon white pepper

1 teaspoon Worcestershire sauce
1 pound sea scallops, quartered
3 tablespoons finely chopped
  parsley
Paprika for garnish

Combine milk, cream, butter, salt, pepper and Worcestershire sauce in a stockpot. Heat to a simmer, stirring frequently. Add scallops and cook 10 minutes or until tender. Garnish individual servings with parsley and paprika.

Yield: 4 servings

"Some Like It Hot" Chili

2 pounds ground sirloin
2 pounds beef stew meat, cubed
3 cups coarsely chopped onions
2 garlic cloves, minced
3-4 jalapeño peppers, minced
2 bell peppers, chopped
2 (28-ounce) cans whole peeled
  tomatoes
1 cup tomato purée

1 (6-ounce) can tomato paste
¼ cup chili powder
2 tablespoons ground cumin
1 tablespoon dried oregano
2 teaspoons ground coriander
Salt and pepper to taste
2 (16-ounce) cans red kidney beans,
  rinsed and drained

Brown meat with onions, garlic, peppers and bell peppers in a stockpot. Add tomatoes and coarsely cut with a spatula. Add tomato purée, tomato paste, chili powder, cumin, oregano, coriander, salt and pepper. Cover and simmer 2 hours, 30 minutes, stirring occasionally. Add beans and simmer an additional 45 minutes. Add more chili powder or cumin for a hotter taste.

Yield: 8 servings

Kidney beans may be omitted for a meat only chili.

Mulligatawny Soup

¼ cup finely chopped onion
1½ teaspoons curry powder
2 tablespoons vegetable oil
1 tart apple, peeled and chopped
¼ cup chopped carrots
¼ cup chopped celery
2 tablespoons chopped sweet red
   pepper
3 tablespoons all-purpose flour
4 cups chicken broth

1 (16-ounce) can tomatoes,
   chopped with juice
1 tablespoon chopped parsley
2 teaspoons lemon juice
1 teaspoon sugar
2 whole cloves
¼ teaspoon salt
Dash of pepper
1 cup diced cooked chicken

Cook onions and curry in oil until onion is tender. Add apples, carrots, celery and peppers. Cook and stir 5 minutes until vegetables are crisp-tender. Sprinkle with flour. Stir to mix well. Add broth, tomatoes, parsley, juice, sugar, cloves, salt and pepper. Bring to boil. Add chicken. Reduce heat and simmer 30 minutes, stirring occasionally.

Yield: 8 servings

Golden Vidalia Cream Soup

2 medium carrots, peeled and sliced
3 medium Vidalia onions, chopped
3 tablespoons butter
1 cup half-and-half

2 teaspoons lemon zest
Salt to taste
Lemon curls for garnish

Place carrots in saucepan and cover with water. Bring to boil. Reduce heat and simmer until tender. Sauté onions in butter. Place carrots, cooking water and onions in a food processor. Purée until smooth. If necessary, add more water. Refrigerate. When ready to serve, stir in half-and-half and zest. Ladle into small chilled bowls. Garnish with lemon curls.

Yield: 4 servings

Aunt Sheila's Gazpacho

4 large tomatoes, peeled or
    unpeeled
½ cucumber, peeled
¼ cup chopped bell pepper
Dash of Tabasco sauce
¼ cup olive oil

4 teaspoons wine vinegar
1 cup tomato juice or tomato
    cocktail juice
½ teaspoon salt
1 teaspoon minced onion
Pepper to taste

Combine tomatoes, cucumber, bell peppers, Tabasco, oil, vinegar, tomato juice, salt, onion and pepper in a blender. Process until smooth. To serve, place soup in a chilled cup and place an ice cube in the center. Serve with extra chopped cucumber, extra tomatoes, croutons, chopped chives or parsley on the side. A dollop of sour cream can also be added to each bowl.

Yield: 4 to 6 servings

Peter Rabbit's Carrot Soup

2 tablespoons butter
1 cup chopped onion
1 teaspoon curry powder
1½ teaspoons salt
¼ teaspoon pepper
2 (14½-ounce) cans chicken broth

2 pounds carrots, peeled and cut
    into 1-inch chunks
3 cups water
1-2 tablespoons lemon juice
2 tablespoons coarsely chopped
    parsley

Melt butter in a 4 to 5-quart stockpot. Sauté onions, curry, salt and pepper 5 minutes until tender. Add broth, carrots and water. Bring to boil. Reduce heat and simmer 20 minutes until carrots are tender. Purée soup in batches in a blender until smooth. Transfer to a saucepan. Add more water to reach desired consistency. Stir in juice. Serve and garnish with parsley.

Yield: 4 servings

Onion Soup

6 medium onions, thinly
    sliced and cut
6 tablespoons butter
6 cups beef broth
1 cup red wine

1 teaspoon dried marjoram
French bread, sliced
Shredded Swiss cheese
Parmesan cheese

Sauté onions in butter until tender. Add broth, wine and marjoram. Bring to boil. Reduce heat and simmer 30 minutes. Ladle soup into bowls. Add a slice of bread and Swiss cheese on top of bread. Pour a small amount of soup over cheese. Sprinkle with Parmesan cheese.

Yield: 6 servings

Creamy Cauliflower Soup

1 head cauliflower, cut into florets
2 tablespoons vegetable oil
1 teaspoon salt
1 tablespoon butter
3 onions, sliced 1-inch thick

1½ teaspoons curry powder
4 cups water
2 cups chicken or vegetable broth
1 teaspoon salt
2 tablespoons chopped parsley

Toss cauliflower with oil and 1 teaspoon salt. Spread out onto a baking sheet. Roast at 450 degrees 25 minutes until browned. Melt butter in a saucepan. Sauté onions until soft. Add curry, roasted cauliflower, water and broth. Cover and bring to boil. Uncover, reduce heat and simmer 5 minutes. Using a slotted spoon, transfer 3 cups cauliflower to a bowl and set aside. Place remaining florets into a blender. Add 1 teaspoon salt and process until smooth. Stir purée into the broth and reheat. Ladle soup into bowls and top with reserved florets and parsley.

Yield: 6 servings

Roasted Eggplant and Garlic Soup

RED PEPPER CREAM

2 sweet red peppers	Salt and pepper to taste
½ cup heavy cream	

Roast peppers in the oven until skin is charred. Cool in a paper bag. Slip off the skins and chop peppers. Combine peppers and cream in a food processor. Process until smooth. Add salt and pepper. Set aside.

SOUP

2 medium eggplant	Salt and pepper to taste
2 heads garlic	4 cups chicken broth
1 onion, chopped	2 cups heavy cream
4 tablespoons butter	

Roast eggplant in the oven until skin is charred. Peel skin and coarsely chop. Roast garlic until soft. Squeeze cloves from skin. Sauté eggplant, garlic and onions in butter 20 minutes in a saucepan. Add salt and pepper. Stir in broth and simmer 20 minutes. Process mixture in batches in a blender until smooth. Transfer to a saucepan. Add cream and slowly heat through. Ladle soup into serving bowls. Drizzle red pepper cream in the center of soup. Pull a toothpick through the cream from the center to the outer edge of the bowls to form a spoke design.

Yield: 8 servings

Roquefort and Walnut Butternut Soup

1½ cups chopped onions
2 tablespoons butter
2½ cups peeled butternut
    squash, cubed
1 teaspoon dried sage

1 teaspoon dried thyme
4 cups chicken broth
Dash of cayenne pepper
¼ cup crumbled Roquefort
½ cup chopped walnuts

Sauté onions in butter 10 minutes until tender. Add squash, sage, thyme and broth. Bring to boil. Reduce heat and simmer 20 to 30 minutes or until squash is tender. Transfer mixture to a blender. Purée until smooth. Add cayenne. Reheat soup. Sprinkle with cheese and walnuts. Serve immediately.

Yield: 4 servings

Pumpkin Black Bean Bisque

1 cup chopped yellow onions
3 tablespoons unsalted butter
2 tablespoons chopped ginger
½ teaspoon cinnamon
¼ teaspoon crushed red pepper
1 (24-ounce) jar unsweetened
    applesauce

1 (30-ounce) can pumpkin
7 cups chicken broth
¼ cup maple syrup
Kosher salt to taste
2 cups half-and-half
1 (15-ounce) can black beans,
    rinsed and drained

Sauté onions in butter until tender. Add ginger, cinnamon and red pepper. Stir until blended. Add applesauce, pumpkin, broth, maple syrup and salt. Stir and simmer 3 minutes until combined. Whisk in half-and-half. Heat thoroughly. Ladle into bowls. Top each bowl with one tablespoon black beans.

Yield: 12 servings

Creamy Spinach Soup

2 tablespoons butter
2 tablespoons minced shallots
1 small leek, thinly sliced
1 pound baby spinach
4 cups vegetable broth

½ cup heavy cream
1 teaspoon curry powder
1 tablespoon lemon juice
Salt and pepper to taste

Melt butter in large stockpot over medium heat. Sauté shallots and leeks about 5 to 10 minutes until tender. Increase heat to high. Add spinach and broth. Cook about 5 minutes until spinach wilts. Purée soup in batches in a food processor. Return purée to pan. Add cream and curry. Gently reheat soup but do not boil. Stir in lemon juice, salt and pepper.

Yield: 4 to 6 servings

Chickpea Soup

1 tablespoon olive oil
2 garlic cloves, minced
1 (14-ounce) can chicken or
   vegetable broth
1¼ cups water
Pepper to taste

1 (15-ounce) can chickpeas, drained
   and rinsed
½ cup ditalini or elbow macaroni,
   cooked al dente
2 tablespoons chopped parsley
2 teaspoons Parmesan cheese

Heat oil in a saucepan. Sauté garlic 2 minutes. Add broth, water and pepper. Bring to boil. Add chickpeas and pasta. Reduce heat and heat thoroughly. Top with parsley and cheese.

Yield: 2 servings

This soup is so delicious so we suggest that you double the recipe!

Moroccan Lentil and Chickpea Soup

1 medium onion, chopped
2 garlic cloves, minced
¼ cup diced sweet red pepper
½ cup chopped carrots
½ cup diced celery
2 tablespoons olive oil
2 teaspoons curry powder
4 saffron threads, crushed in
    ¼ cup boiling water
1 (14½-ounce) can diced tomatoes

6 cups vegetable broth
1 cup water
1 cup lentils, rinsed and drained
½ teaspoon black pepper
1 teaspoon salt
2 tablespoons lemon juice
1 tablespoon ketchup
1 (15½-ounce) can chickpeas,
    drained and rinsed
¼ cup minced parsley

Sauté onions, garlic, peppers, carrots and celery in oil until tender. Add curry and saffron in water, tomatoes, broth, water and lentils. Bring to boil. Add pepper, salt, lemon juice and ketchup. Simmer 20 to 30 minutes or until lentils are tender. Add chickpeas and top with parsley.

Yield: 12 servings

Easy Navy Bean Soup

1 large onion, chopped
2 garlic cloves, minced
3 carrots, sliced
2 stalks celery, sliced
2 tablespoons olive oil
1 tablespoon dried parsley

1 teaspoon pepper
¼ teaspoon salt
4 cups chicken or vegetable broth
3 (15-ounce) cans navy beans,
    drained and rinsed

Sauté onions, garlic, carrots and celery in hot oil 5 minutes, stirring often. Add parsley, pepper, salt, broth and beans. Bring to boil. Reduce heat and simmer 15 to 20 minutes, stirring occasionally.

Yield: 4 servings

Sweet Potato and Tomato Soup

1 cup chopped yellow onions
3 tablespoons butter
2 garlic cloves, minced
1 (14½-ounce) can diced tomatoes
1 (15¾-ounce) can sweet potatoes,
   drained and cubed
1 cup water

⅓ cup tomato paste
1 tablespoon brown sugar
1 teaspoon salt
½ teaspoon pepper
¼ teaspoon cayenne pepper
1 (14-ounce) can chicken broth

Sauté onions in butter until soft. Add garlic and cook 2 minutes. Stir in tomatoes, sweet potatoes, water, tomato paste, brown sugar, salt and pepper. Simmer 20 minutes. Purée soup in batches in food processor. Return purée to pan. Stir in cayenne and broth. Simmer 15 minutes.

Yield: 4 to 6 servings

Tomato Cognac Soup

1 large Spanish onion, chopped
6 tablespoons butter
3 pounds canned, peeled plum
   tomatoes, chopped and
   undrained

1 tablespoon dried basil
2 cups heavy cream
2 tablespoons dark brown sugar
5 tablespoons cognac
Salt and pepper to taste

Sauté onions in butter 20 minutes until tender but not browned. Add tomatoes and liquid. Stir in basil. Bring to boil. Cover, reduce heat and simmer 30 minutes. Set aside and cool slightly. Purée soup in batches in food processor. Heat cream in a large stockpot. Whisk in brown sugar. Add soup purée. Heat thoroughly, but do not boil. Just before serving, add cognac, salt and pepper.

Yield: 6 servings

Honey Mustard Turkey Salad

HONEY MUSTARD DRESSING

½ cup mayonnaise
2 tablespoons honey Dijon mustard

¾ teaspoon soy sauce
¾ teaspoon lemon juice

Whisk together mayonnaise, mustard, soy sauce and juice. Set aside.

SALAD

2 cups chopped cooked turkey
6 slices bacon, cooked and crumbled
¼ cup thin strips sweet red pepper
¼ cup sliced green onions

1 (2-ounce) package roasted cashews
Lettuce leaves
Sweet red pepper rings
Chow Mein noodles

Combine turkey, bacon, pepper strips and onions. Add dressing and toss to coat. Cover and refrigerate. Stir in cashews just before serving. Arrange lettuce and pepper rings on four salad plates. Top with turkey mixture. Sprinkle with noodles.

Yield: 4 servings

Great to make with leftover Thanksgiving turkey!

Cranberry Turkey Salad

1 head red leaf lettuce
12-16 slices cooked turkey
½ cup coarsely chopped pecans
1 cup whole cranberry sauce

2 tablespoons vinegar
1 tablespoon sugar
1 cup crumbled feta cheese
½ cup olive oil

Arrange lettuce on four salad plates. Place 3 to 4 turkey slices on each plate. Sprinkle with pecans. Combine cranberry sauce, vinegar, sugar and half cheese in a blender. While blender is running, slowly add oil through hole in top. Stir in remaining cheese. Drizzle dressing over salad.

Yield: 4 servings

Newport Tuna Salad

2 (6-ounce) cans solid white tuna in water, drained and chunked
½ cup or more mayonnaise
4 tablespoons chopped black olives
2 tablespoons sweet pickle relish
½ cup finely chopped celery
1 hard-cooked egg, chopped

2 teaspoons lemon pepper
2 teaspoons lemon juice
4 medium tomatoes, cored
Curly leaf lettuce
Paprika for garnish
Sliced cucumbers
Italian dressing

Combine tuna, mayonnaise, olives, relish, celery, egg, lemon pepper and juice. Slice tomatoes to the core into quarters. Do not cut all the way through. Tomatoes should be attached on the bottom and opened like a flower. Arrange lettuce on four dinner plates. Place a tomato in the center of each plate. Using an ice cream scoop, scoop tuna salad into center of tomato. Sprinkle with paprika. Garnish with cucumbers. Lightly drizzle dressing over tomato and lettuce.

Yield: 4 servings

This is a wonderful meal for a hot summer night. Oh, do not forget the wavy potato chips!

"Summer afternoon…to me those have always been the two most beautiful words in the English language."
~ Henry James Quoted by Edith Wharton

Tossed Spinach and Pear Salad

DRESSING

½ cup olive oil
2 tablespoons cider vinegar
1 tablespoon Parmesan cheese
1 teaspoon salt
½ teaspoon Worcestershire sauce
¼ small onion

¼ teaspoon sugar
¼ teaspoon dry mustard
¼ teaspoon dried basil
¼ teaspoon dried oregano
¼ teaspoon pepper

Combine oil, vinegar, cheese, salt, Worcestershire sauce, onion, sugar, mustard, basil, oregano and pepper in a blender. Process until smooth. Set aside.

SALAD

1 (10-ounce) bag spinach, washed
    and dried
2 medium pears, peeled and wedged

¼ cup golden raisins
¼ cup blanched slivered
    almonds

Gently combine spinach, pears, raisins and almonds. Pour dressing over salad and toss gently. Serve immediately.

Yield: 6 servings

Autumn Dinner Salad

BALSAMIC VINAIGRETTE

1 teaspoon dry mustard
½ teaspoon seasoned salt
¼ teaspoon pepper
3 tablespoons balsamic vinegar

½ teaspoon onion juice
1 garlic clove, crushed
¼ cup olive oil

Combine mustard, salt and pepper. Stir in vinegar, juice and garlic. Let stand 1 hour. Just before serving, strain dressing to remove garlic. Whisk in oil and set aside.

SALAD

2 tablespoons butter
½ cup chopped walnuts
3 tablespoons packed brown sugar
1 firm pear or apple

Mixed salad greens, rinsed
 and torn
3 green onions, chopped
3-4 ounces crumbled blue cheese

Melt butter in a skillet over medium heat. Add walnuts and sugar. Sauté nuts until softened. Remove from pan and cool. When ready to serve, peel and cut fruit into thin slices. Combine lettuce, fruit, green onions and half the nuts and half the cheese. Toss with vinaigrette. Top with remaining nuts and cheese. Serve immediately.

Yield: 4 to 6 servings

Layered Summer Salad

2 cups pearl barley
6 tablespoons fresh lemon juice
¼ cup white wine vinegar
4 teaspoons Dijon mustard
1½ teaspoons salt
¼ teaspoon pepper
1 tablespoon sugar
½ teaspoon celery seed

1 cup olive oil
2¼ cups thinly sliced celery
1½ cups dried cherries
10 ounces Maytag blue cheese,
  crumbled
1 small head green cabbage,
  thinly shredded
5 large carrots, peeled and grated

Place barley in a stockpot. Add 2 quarts water. Cover and bring to boil. Reduce heat and simmer 40 minutes until tender. Drain and transfer to a glass serving bowl. In a separate bowl, whisk together juice, vinegar, mustard, salt, pepper, sugar and celery seed. Whisk in oil in a steady stream until blended. Drizzle 2 tablespoons dressing over barley. Arrange celery over barley and drizzle with 2 tablespoons dressing. Top with cherries and drizzle with 2 tablespoons dressing. Crumble half the cheese over cherries and drizzle with 2 tablespoons dressing. In another bowl, toss cabbage with 3 tablespoons dressing. Spread cabbage over cheese. Layer carrots over cabbage and drizzle with remaining dressing. Cover and refrigerate 24 hours. Top with remaining cheese. Serve at room temperature.

Yield: 8 to 10 servings

*"Summertime is important. It's like a shaft of sunlight.
Or a note in music. Or the way the back of a
baby's neck smells if its mother keeps it tidy."*
~ STUART LITTLE

Million Dollar Salad

½ head butter lettuce, finely chopped
½ head romaine lettuce, finely chopped
½ bunch watercress, finely chopped
1 small bunch chicory, finely chopped

2 medium tomatoes, finely chopped
2 cups cooked diced chicken
6 slices bacon, cooked and crumbled
3 hard-cooked eggs, chopped
2 tablespoons chopped chives
3 ounces Maytag blue cheese, crumbled

Arrange all lettuce, watercress and chicory in a salad bowl. Scatter tomatoes, chicken and bacon over greens. Top with eggs, chives and cheese. Just before serving, toss with your favorite dressing.

Yield: 4 servings

Strawberry Romaine Salad

1 cup extra-virgin olive oil
¾ cup sugar
½ cup red wine vinegar
2 garlic cloves, minced
½ teaspoon salt
¼ teaspoon white pepper
½ teaspoon paprika

1 head romaine lettuce
1 head Boston lettuce
1 pint strawberries, sliced
1 cup shredded Monterey Jack cheese
½ cup toasted walnuts

Whisk together oil, sugar, vinegar, garlic, salt, pepper and paprika until smooth. Combine lettuce, strawberries, cheese and walnuts in a large bowl. Pour on dressing and toss to coat. Dressing may be refrigerated up to 1 week.

Yield: 12 servings

Recipe may be halved for smaller groups. During the month of June, we love to take advantage of the fresh strawberries. Usually, we have a special gathering on the night of the Strawberry Moon. All of the recipes we serve have strawberries in them.

Pink and Green Salad with Maple-Balsamic Dressing

MAPLE-BALSAMIC DRESSING

¼ cup balsamic vinegar	2 tablespoons water
¼ cup maple syrup	½ teaspoon salt
1 garlic clove, minced	¼ teaspoon pepper
¼ teaspoon Dijon mustard	1 cup extra-virgin olive oil

Combine vinegar, syrup, garlic, mustard, water, salt and pepper. Slowly whisk in oil. Store in the refrigerator for up to 1 month. Bring to room temperature and shake well before serving.

SALAD

White kale, torn	Belgian endive, torn
Purple kale, torn	Red Belgian endive, torn
Feathery mizuna, torn	Baby spinach, torn

Arrange colorful greens on pink or green Depression glass plates. Drizzle with dressing.

Yield: 6 to 8 servings

Broccoli Salad

½ cup olive oil
2 packages oriental flavored
   noodles, broken into bite-size
   pieces
½ bunch chopped green onions
½ cup sliced almonds

¼ cup sugar
1 package oriental seasoning, from
   noodles
¼ cup cider vinegar
1 (12-ounce) package broccoli slaw

Combine oil, noodles, green onions and almonds in a saucepan. Sauté until noodles are lightly browned. In a bowl, combine sugar, seasoning packet and vinegar. Mix well. Remove noodle mixture from heat. Place in a serving bowl. Add broccoli and seasoning mixture. Mix well to coat. Refrigerate.

Yield: 4 to 6 servings

The oriental noodles and seasoning are actually a soup found in the super market. For a crowd, this recipe can be doubled.

Vidalia Beet Salad

4 medium beets, cooked and
   peeled
1 large Vidalia onion
¼ cup olive oil
¼ cup vegetable oil

¼ cup cider vinegar
¼ teaspoon celery seeds, crushed
¼ teaspoon dry mustard
¼ teaspoon paprika
Salt to taste

Cut beets and onions in a ¼-inch dice. Combine both oils and vinegar in a jar. Add crushed celery seeds, mustard and paprika to oil. Seal lid and shake well. Pour over beets and onions. Mix thoroughly. Refrigerate 2 hours, stirring occasionally. Bring to room temperature. Add salt and serve.

Yield: 6 servings

Armenian Cucumber Salad

1 pound Armenia cucumbers,
    coarsely chopped
1 large red onion, thinly sliced
2 tomatoes, quartered
1 teaspoon dried oregano

½ cup extra-virgin olive oil
½ cup red wine vinegar
1 tablespoon honey
1 cup toasted Italian bread, cubed
Salt and pepper to taste

Combine cucumbers, onions, tomatoes and oregano. Set aside. In a separate bowl, whisk together oil, vinegar and honey. Pour ¾ cup dressing over cucumber mixture. Refrigerate 1 hour. To serve, stir mixture and divide equally onto four salad plates. Top with bread cubes and sprinkle with salt and pepper. Drizzle with more dressing if desired.

Yield: 4 servings

Armenian cucumbers may be found at local farm stands during the summer months in the Northeast. English cucumbers are a fine substitution.

Chickpea and Feta Salad

2 (19-ounce) cans chickpeas,
    drained and rinsed
2 large tomatoes, diced
6 ounces feta cheese, crumbled
3 green onions, thinly sliced
6 kalamata olives, pitted and
    quartered

2 tablespoons chopped parsley
½ cup olive oil
1 tablespoon red wine vinegar
1 teaspoon dried oregano
½ teaspoon pepper

Combine chickpeas, tomatoes, cheese, onions, olives and parsley in a serving bowl. Whisk together oil, vinegar, oregano and pepper. Pour over salad. Toss gently to coat. Serve at room temperature.

Yield: 6 to 8 servings

Green Bean, Yellow Bean and Cherry Tomato Salad

¾ pound green beans, trimmed
¾ pound yellow wax beans, trimmed
3 cups cherry tomatoes
1 medium red onion, thinly sliced

1½ cups thinly sliced basil
5 tablespoons extra-virgin olive oil
3 tablespoons red wine vinegar
¼ teaspoon sugar
Salt and pepper to taste

Cook beans in a large pot of salted boiling water 5 minutes or until crisp-tender. Drain and rinse with cold water. Combine beans, tomatoes, onions and basil in serving bowl. Whisk together oil, vinegar, sugar, salt and pepper. Add dressing to vegetables and toss to coat. Cover and refrigerate at least 1 hour or up to 4 hours, tossing occasionally. Serve cold or room temperature.

Yield: 6 to 8 servings

Refreshing, colorful and delicious.

Broccoli Slaw

½ cup mayonnaise
2 teaspoons sugar
2 tablespoons cider vinegar
1 tablespoon soy sauce
1 teaspoon celery seed
1 (12-ounce) bag broccoli slaw

2 teaspoons minced garlic
1 tablespoon minced Vidalia onion
3 tablespoons pine nuts, toasted
½ cup raisins or thinly sliced red apple (optional)

Blend mayonnaise, sugar, vinegar, soy sauce and celery seed. Set aside. Combine slaw, garlic and onions in a serving bowl. Pour on dressing and toss to coat. Add raisins. Cover and refrigerate several hours. Top with nuts prior to serving.

Yield: 6 servings

Red, White and Blue Coleslaw

1 medium head red cabbage, shredded
½ pound blue seedless grapes, halved
1 cup chopped parsley

¼ cup crumbled Maytag blue cheese
¾ cup mayonnaise
2 tablespoons sugar
2 tablespoons cider vinegar
¼ cup Dijon mustard

Combine cabbage, grapes, parsley and cheese in a serving bowl. Whisk together mayonnaise, sugar, vinegar and mustard. Pour over slaw and toss to coat. Cover and refrigerate at least 2 hours. Sprinkle with more cheese and garnish with blue grapes if desired.

Yield: 12 to 16 servings

Early Spring Maple Slaw

1½ teaspoons Dijon mustard
2 tablespoons corn oil
3 tablespoons cider vinegar
3 tablespoons maple syrup
1 garlic clove, minced
1 teaspoon salt

¾ cup finely diced onion
1 green bell pepper, cut julienne
1 large carrot, shredded
6 cups thinly shredded cabbage, half red and half green

Whisk together mustard, oil, vinegar, syrup, garlic and salt in a large bowl. Stir in onions. Let stand 10 minutes to marinate. Add peppers, carrots and cabbage. Mix well to coat. Let stand 15 minutes, stirring occasionally.

Yield: 6 servings

Coleslaw

½ cup mayonnaise
2 tablespoons sugar
2 tablespoons cider vinegar
¾ teaspoon salt
¼ teaspoon dry mustard

1⅛ teaspoons celery seeds
4 cups shredded cabbage
¾ cup shredded carrots
½ cup diced bell peppers
2 tablespoons sliced green onions

Whisk mayonnaise, sugar, vinegar, salt, mustard and celery seeds. Combine cabbage, carrots, peppers and green onions. Pour dressing over vegetables and mix well. Refrigerate at least 2 hours or more before serving. May add red and yellow peppers.

Yield: 8 servings

Mango Jalapeño Slaw

½ head green cabbage, shredded
2 jalapeño peppers, minced
Salt and pepper to taste
3 tablespoons balsamic vinegar

¾ cup mayonnaise
1 ripe mango, peeled, seeded
   and cubed

Combine cabbage, jalapeño peppers, salt and pepper. Blend vinegar and mayonnaise. Stir into cabbage. Gently fold in mango. Refrigerate until ready to serve.

Yield: 6 to 8 servings

Cole Porter Slaw

1 (12-ounce) package coleslaw mix	⅓ cup diced red onions
⅓ cup bottled Greek salad dressing	4 ounces crumbled feta cheese
⅓ cup kalamata olives	

Combine slaw, dressing, olives and onions. Fold in cheese. Mix well. Let stand 30 minutes. Add more dressing and olives if desired.

Yield: 6 servings

"It's delightful, it's delicious, it's de-lovely."

~ COLE PORTER

Aunt Pat's Bing Cherry Salad

1 (16-ounce) can Bing cherries, drained and juice reserved	6 ounces cream cheese, softened
2 (3-ounce) packages cherry flavored gelatin	2 cups crushed pineapple, drained
	1 cup chopped walnuts
	1 (12-ounce) Coke

Heat cherry juice in a pan. Whisk in gelatin until dissolved. Add cream cheese and stir until smooth. Add pineapple, walnuts and Coke. Pour into a mold. Refrigerate.

Yield: 8 to 10 servings

Our Southern Aunt brought this recipe into our family over 45 years ago. It has been a holiday favorite ever since.

Cranberry Salad Ring

1 (6-ounce) package cranberry
    flavored gelatin
1 cup boiling water
¼ cup sugar
1 tablespoon lemon juice
1 cup pineapple juice

1 cup chopped fresh cranberries
1 cup crushed pineapple, drained
1 orange, seeded and coarsely
    chopped
½ cup finely chopped walnuts

Dissolve gelatin in water. Add sugar, lemon juice and pineapple juice. Stir well. Add cranberries, pineapple, oranges and walnuts. Pour mixture into a mold. Refrigerate at least 8 hours or overnight.

Yield: 8 to 10 servings

Fresh Fruit Salad

½ cup honey
Juice of 2 limes
1 ripe mango, peeled and diced
½ pint blueberries
½ pint raspberries

½ pint blackberries
½ pint strawberries, sliced
2 kiwi, peeled, sliced into rounds
    and quartered

Heat honey and juice until dissolved. Place mango, all berries and kiwi in a large crystal bowl. Pour honey mixture over fruit. Let stand 5 minutes.

Yield: 10 servings

Great when served at a brunch or shower.

Fresh Pineapple Salad

1 head red leaf lettuce, rinsed and patted dry

1 pineapple, cored and sliced into ½-inch rings

1 Bermuda onion, cut into ¼-inch slices

2 large Beefsteak tomatoes, sliced into ½-inch slices

Salt and pepper to taste

8-ounces Maytag blue cheese, crumbled

Extra-virgin olive oil

Balsamic vinegar

Arrange lettuce leaves on four salad plates. Place one pineapple slice on each plate. Top with an onion slice and tomato slice. Sprinkle with salt and pepper. Top with blue cheese and drizzle with oil and vinegar.

Yield: 4 servings

Roasted Sweet Potato Salad

DRESSING

½ cup olive oil

2 tablespoons orange juice concentrate, undiluted

1 teaspoon ground cumin

Whisk together oil, juice concentrate and cumin. Set aside.

POTATO SALAD

4 cups peeled and diced sweet potatoes

½ cup olive oil

3 garlic cloves, minced

2 teaspoons dried thyme

Salt and pepper to taste

1 cup dried cranberries

1 cup diced celery

1 bunch parsley, minced

Combine potatoes, oil, garlic, thyme, salt and pepper in a roasting pan. Toss to coat. Roast potatoes at 400 degrees 45 minutes or until crusty and fork tender. Cool. Combine potatoes, cranberries, celery and parsley. Pour dressing over potatoes and toss to coat. Serve at room temperature.

Yield: 6 servings

Tomato, Watermelon and Cucumber Salad

2 large tomatoes, cut into 1-inch
    wedges
2 pound watermelon, cut into
    ½ x 2-inch pieces
1 cucumber, peeled, seeded and cut
    into ½-inch wedges
½ small onion, thinly sliced

3 tablespoons red wine vinegar
2 tablespoons extra-virgin
    olive oil
1 teaspoon salt
¼ teaspoon pepper
¼ cup sliced basil

Combine tomatoes, watermelon, cucumbers and onions. Whisk together vinegar, oil, salt and pepper. Pour dressing over melon mixture. Gently toss to coat. Cover and refrigerate up to 2 hours. Sprinkle with basil.

Yield: 10 to 12 servings

Our cousin Robin brought this recipe over one summer evening. We loved it the moment we tasted it.

Summer Potato Salad

4 cups cooked new potatoes, cut
    into ½-inch pieces
½ cup chopped sweet red peppers
½ cup chopped bell peppers
½ cup chopped yellow peppers
¼ cup chopped celery
¼ cup chopped red onions
¼ cup chopped chives

2 tablespoons chopped flat-leaf
    parsley
¼ cup vegetable oil
2 tablespoons red wine vinegar
1 tablespoon chopped thyme
    or 1 teaspoon dried
Salt and pepper to taste

Combine potatoes, all peppers, celery, onions, chives and parsley in a large bowl. Gently mix. Whisk together oil, vinegar, thyme, salt and pepper. Pour dressing over potato mixture. Toss gently to coat. Serve at room temperature.

Yield: 12 servings

Mustard Vinaigrette

½ cup tarragon vinegar
½ cup Dijon mustard
1½ cups olive oil
Salt and pepper to taste

1½ shallots, finely minced
1 tablespoon chopped parsley
1 tablespoon chopped tarragon

Whisk together vinegar and mustard. Slowly whisk in oil. Add salt, pepper, shallots, parsley and tarragon. Mix well before using.

Yield: 2½ cups

An Easter favorite when served over steamed asparagus.

Fattoosh

2 loaves Syrian bread, toasted
1 small head lettuce, chopped
1 cucumber, chopped
3 tomatoes, diced
1 bunch radishes, sliced
1 bunch green onions or
    1 large sweet onion, diced

1 cup chopped parsley
1 teaspoon dried mint or
    ½ cup fresh, chopped
1 garlic clove, crushed
2 tablespoons olive oil
2 tablespoons lemon juice
Salt and pepper to taste

Break bread into small pieces. Place in a large serving bowl. Add lettuce, cucumbers, tomatoes, radishes, green onions, parsley, mint and garlic. Whisk together oil, juice, salt and pepper. Pour dressing over salad and toss to coat.

Yield: 6 servings

Wonderful when summertime garden vegetables can be used. If desired, you can add more oil and lemon juice.

Honey Vinaigrette Salad

Mixed greens
Red or green pears, diced
Dried cherries
Cucumbers, sliced (optional)
Blue cheese

Pepper, garlic powder and celery
    salt to taste
⅔ cup vegetable oil
2 tablespoons vinegar
2-3 tablespoons honey

Combine greens, pears, cherries, cucumbers, cheese, pepper, garlic powder and celery salt. Mix well. Whisk together oil, vinegar and honey. Pour dressing over salad and toss to coat.

Yield: 6 servings

Maple Dijon Cream Salad Dressing

¼ cup extra-virgin olive oil
½ cup vegetable oil
2½ tablespoons Dijon mustard
3 tablespoons maple syrup

2 tablespoons balsamic vinegar
¼ cup half-and-half
Dash of salt
1 garlic clove, scored

Whisk together olive oil, vegetable oil, mustard, syrup, vinegar, half-and-half and salt. Add garlic and refrigerate at least 1 hour.

Yield: 1 cup

Serve over a salad of baby greens, crumbled Gorgonzola cheese, chopped pecans, sliced pears, chopped apples or cranberries.

Notes

Vegetables & Sides

"In my garden, after a rainfall, you can faintly, yes, hear the breaking of new blooms."

~ TRUMAN CAPOTE

Oven Roasted Asparagus

1½ pounds asparagus, trimmed
2 tablespoons olive oil

Kosher salt and pepper to taste

Toss asparagus with oil. Sprinkle with salt and pepper. Place in a single layer on a baking sheet. Roast at 425 degrees 15 to 20 minutes or until tender and browned.

Yield: 6 servings

Green Beans with Garlic

1 pound green beans, trimmed
2 tablespoons butter

1 garlic clove, minced
2 tablespoons Parmesan cheese

Steam beans until tender. Melt butter in a small saucepan. Sauté garlic 2 to 3 minutes until tender. Pour garlic butter over beans. Stir to coat. Sprinkle with cheese. Toss gently.

Yield: 6 servings

Stir-Fried Asparagus

1½ pounds asparagus, trimmed
½ cup chicken broth
1 teaspoon salt
2 tablespoons soy sauce

1 teaspoon sugar
1 tablespoon peanut oil
1 tablespoon cornstarch

Cut asparagus on the diagonal to 1-inch length. Parboil asparagus in boiling water 2 to 4 minutes. Cool under cold water. Drain well. Combine broth, salt, soy sauce, sugar and oil in a skillet. Stir-fry asparagus in mixture 1 minute. Add cornstarch. Stir until sauce thickens.

Yield: 6 servings

String Bean Stew

3 tablespoons butter
2 pounds boneless lamb, cut
    into 2-inch cubes
1 teaspoon salt
⅛ teaspoon pepper

1 large onion, sliced
1½ cups water
½ cup canned tomato sauce
1 pound French cut string beans

Melt butter in saucepan. Add lamb, salt and pepper. Cook until meat is browned. Add onions and cook until tender. Add water and bring to boil. Reduce heat, cover and simmer 1 hour, 15 minutes. Add tomato sauce and beans. Mix well and cover. Simmer 30 minutes longer.

Yield: 6 servings

We can vividly recall seeing this cooking on our grandmother's stove. It is a real treat. It was traditionally served with rice pilaf.

Baby Lima Beans

1 (10-ounce) package frozen baby
    lima beans
2 tablespoons olive oil
2 medium celery stalks with leaves,
    finely chopped
1 small red onion, finely chopped

1 large garlic clove, minced
1 tablespoon white wine vinegar
2 teaspoons minced parsley
¼ teaspoon salt
⅛ teaspoon pepper

Prepare lima beans according to package directions. Drain and set aside. Heat oil in a skillet. Sauté celery, onions and garlic 10 minutes or until tender, stirring occasionally. Add lima beans, vinegar, parsley, salt and pepper. Heat thoroughly.

Yield: 4 servings

Pete's Vegetarian Baked Beans

1 (1-pound) package white navy
    beans
3 tablespoons packed brown sugar
6 -7 tablespoons molasses

1 tablespoon dry mustard
½ cup ketchup
4 tablespoons butter
1 onion, chopped

Soak beans overnight or use quick method. Drain and place in a bean pot. Add brown sugar, molasses, mustard, ketchup, butter and onions. Cover with water. Place pot in a 325 degree oven. Bake about 7 hours until soft but not mushy.

Yield: 12 servings

Invite your family to bring over their bean pots and beans. You might as well bake several pots at one time. At the end of the day, have them return to pick up their freshly made baked beans!

Black and White Bean Salad

1 (19-ounce) can cannelloni beans,
    drained and rinsed
1 (19-ounce) can black beans,
    drained and rinsed
½ pound cherry tomatoes, quartered

½ cup basil leaves, torn into
    ½-inch pieces
1 teaspoon course salt
Freshly ground pepper
¼ cup olive oil
3 garlic cloves, minced

Combine cannelloni beans, black beans, tomatoes, basil and salt in a bowl. Sprinkle with pepper. Add oil and garlic and gently toss to coat. Let stand 30 minutes before serving. Serve at room temperature.

Yield: 6 servings

Spicy Broccoli

2 garlic cloves, slivered
½ cup olive oil
1½ pounds broccoli
½ cup water
½ teaspoon salt

½ teaspoon crushed red pepper
2 medium tomatoes, diced
4 slices bacon, cut into ½-inch
    pieces cooked and crumbled
⅓ cup sliced almonds

Sauté garlic in oil until tender. Add broccoli, water, salt and red pepper. Cover and cook 5 minutes. Remove cover and cook 2 more minutes until broccoli is tender. Add tomatoes, bacon and almonds. Toss gently. Heat to warm tomatoes but do not cook to release liquid. Transfer to a serving bowl and serve immediately.

Yield: 6 servings

Roasted Cauliflower

1 large cauliflower
2 tablespoons vegetable oil
1 teaspoon salt

½ teaspoon pepper
½ teaspoon garlic powder

Combine cauliflower, oil, salt, pepper and garlic powder. Toss well to coat. Place cauliflower on a large baking sheet. Bake at 450 degrees 30 minutes or until florets are browned.

Yield: 6 servings

May also replace the cauliflower with broccoli or use a combination of both! Delicious!

Christmas Brussels Sprouts

1 pound Brussels sprouts, steamed	½ teaspoon Dijon mustard
3 tablespoons maple syrup	¼ teaspoon salt
1 tablespoon vegetable oil	¼ teaspoon pepper
1 tablespoon apple cider vinegar	¼ cup dried cranberries

Coat baking dish with cooking spray. Arrange Brussels sprouts on bottom of dish. Whisk together syrup, oil, vinegar, mustard, salt and pepper. Pour over sprouts. Top with cranberries. Cover and bake at 375 degrees 30 minutes.

Yield: 4 servings

Recipe can easily be doubled. If you are unable to find fresh Brussels sprouts, you may use frozen ones that have been thawed. Decrease the cooking time by 10 minutes. The green of the Brussels sprouts and the red cranberries compliment the holiday table.

6 Carat Lyonnaise

1 chicken bouillon	1 tablespoon all-purpose flour
½ cup boiling water	¼ teaspoon salt
6 medium carrots, peeled and cut into julienne strips	Dash of pepper
	¾ cup water
4 tablespoons butter	Dash of sugar
3 medium onions, sliced	

Dissolve bouillon in water. Cook carrots in broth 10 minutes. Set aside. Melt butter in a skillet. Add onions and cover. Cook 10 minutes, stirring occasionally. Stir in flour, salt, pepper and water. Bring to boil. Add carrots with liquid. Simmer, uncovered, 10 minutes. Stir in sugar.

Yield: 6 servings

Glazed Brussels Sprouts and Carrots

½ cup water
1 cup halved Brussels sprouts
2 medium carrots, sliced
1 teaspoon cornstarch

½ teaspoon sugar
¼ teaspoon salt (optional)
⅛ teaspoon ground nutmeg
⅓ cup orange juice

Bring water to boil. Add sprouts and carrots. Cover and simmer 6 to 8 minutes. Drain and return to pan. Whisk together cornstarch, sugar, salt, nutmeg and juice until smooth. Pour over vegetables. Bring to boil. Cook and stir 2 minutes. Serve immediately.

Yield: 4 servings

This could be a great addition to your Easter dinner.

24-Karat Carrots

4 cups sliced carrots
3 tablespoons butter
3 tablespoons olive oil

1½ cups milk
1 package onion soup mix
2 tablespoons all-purpose flour

Sauté carrots in butter and oil until lightly browned. Add milk. Blend soup mix and flour. Add to carrots and cook 3 to 4 minutes until thickened. Pour mixture into a 2-quart baking dish. Cover and bake at 350 degrees 40 to 50 minutes until tender.

Yield: 6 to 8 servings

Cranberry and Dried Fruit Relish

1 (12-ounce) package fresh or
  frozen cranberries
1 cup dried fruit (a combination of
  cherries, blueberries, golden
  raisins or dried peaches)

1 cup sugar
2 cups water

Combine cranberries, fruit, sugar and water. Bring to boil. Reduce heat and simmer 15 to 20 minutes until cranberries burst and liquid is syrupy. Store in a covered container in the refrigerator. Bring to room temperature before serving. Serve with your favorite autumn or holiday meal.

Yield: 8 servings

This relish compliments poultry, game and pork.

Honey Glazed Brandied Carrots

1 (1-pound) package baby carrots
3 tablespoons butter
3 tablespoons honey

2 tablespoons brandy
1½ tablespoons chopped parsley
Salt and pepper to taste

Cook carrots in salted boiling water until tender. Drain. Transfer to a skillet. Add butter, honey, brandy, parsley, salt and pepper. Cook and stir until glazed and glossy.

Yield: 6 servings

Apple and Onion Casserole

4 medium onions, sliced
4 tablespoons butter
Salt and pepper to taste

4 apples, peeled and sliced
Sugar and cinnamon mixture

Parboil onions 10 minutes. Drain. Save ⅓ cup cooking liquid. Layer onions in a buttered 11 x 7 x 2-inch baking dish. Dot with butter and sprinkle with salt and pepper. Layer apples over onions. Dot with butter and sprinkle with sugar mixture. Repeat layers in same fashion. Pour cooking liquid on top. Bake at 350 degrees 45 minutes to 1 hour.

Yield: 6 to 8 servings

Carrot and Turnip Mash

1 (1-pound) package carrots,
    peeled and diced
1 pound turnip, peeled and diced

4 tablespoons butter
Salt and pepper to taste

Boil carrots and turnips until tender. Strain. Transfer to a bowl. Add butter, salt and pepper. Mix until well blended. Mixture will not be smooth unless you purée in a food processor.

Yield: 6 servings

*"Don't go into Mr. McGregor's garden: Your Father
had an accident there; and was put in a pie by Mrs. McGregor."*
~ THE TALE OF PETER RABBIT

Sautéed Mushrooms

2 tablespoons butter
1 tablespoon olive oil
1 shallot, minced
1½ pounds small white
    mushrooms, halved

Coarse salt and pepper to taste
½ teaspoon garlic powder
¼ cup dry red wine

Melt butter with oil in a large skillet. Sauté shallot 5 minutes until soft. Increase heat and add mushrooms, salt, pepper and garlic powder. Cover and cook 5 minutes until mushrooms release their liquid. Uncover and increase heat to high. Cook and stir until liquid evaporates and mushrooms are browned. Add wine and cook until absorbed. Serve hot.

Yield: 8 servings

Vidalia Onion Pie

1 cup butter cracker crumbs
4 tablespoons butter, melted
2 cups thinly sliced Vidalia onions
2 tablespoons butter
2 eggs
¾ cup milk

¾ teaspoon salt
Dash of coarse pepper
¼ cup shredded sharp
    Cheddar cheese
Paprika and parsley to taste

Combine cracker crumbs with butter. Press into an 8-inch pie plate. Sauté onions in butter until tender. Spoon over crust. Beat eggs, milk, salt and pepper. Pour mixture over onions. Sprinkle with cheese and paprika. Bake at 350 degrees 30 minutes or until tester comes out clean. Top with parsley.

Yield: 8 servings

This recipe has been served at our Mother's Day Brunch! Everyone enjoyed the Vidalia Onion Pie!

Cranberry Applesauce

4 large cooking apples, peeled
  and cut into chunks
1 cup fresh or frozen
  cranberries

¾ cup sugar
1 cup water
¼ teaspoon ground cloves
½ teaspoon cinnamon

Combine apples, cranberries, sugar, water, cloves and cinnamon in a 4-quart saucepan. Bring to boil. Reduce heat. Cover and simmer 15 to 20 minutes until cranberries pop. Place mixture in a food processor. Blend until smooth. Serve warm or cold.

Yield: 4 cups

This side dish adds color and texture to any meal. Cranberry Applesauce is a great addition to pork, poultry or game.

Southern Vidalia Onion Squares

1 egg, beaten
¾ cup milk
2 cups biscuit baking mix
2 tablespoons poppy seeds
2 cups chopped Vidalia onions
2 tablespoons butter

1 egg
¾ cup sour cream
½ teaspoon salt
¼ teaspoon pepper
Paprika to taste

Blend egg, milk, baking mix and poppy seeds. Press mixture into a greased 9 x 9 x 2-inch square baking dish. Sauté onions in butter until tender and browned. Spread over dough. Beat egg with sour cream, salt and pepper. Pour over onions. Bake at 400 degrees 25 minutes. Cool slightly and cut into squares. Sprinkle with paprika.

Yield: 6 servings

Roasted Vidalia Onions

4 Vidalia onions
5 tablespoons olive oil
2 tablespoons red wine vinegar

1 teaspoon Creole mustard
Salt and pepper to taste

Brush onion skin with oil and place them in a pie pan. Roast at 400 degrees 1 hour. Remove from oven and cool. With a sharp knife, split open. Discard skin and score the inside of onion. Whisk together oil, vinegar, mustard, salt and pepper. Pour over onions and serve.

Yield: 4 to 6 servings

Mommy's Spanish Peppers

3 tablespoons olive oil
4 bell peppers, cut into
    1¼-inch strips
2 sweet red peppers, cut into
    1¼-inch strips

4 whole garlic cloves
Salt and pepper to taste
1 (6-ounce) can tomato paste
1½ cups water

Heat oil in a large skillet. Sauté peppers and garlic until tender. Add salt and pepper. Whisk together tomato paste and water. Pour sauce over vegetables. Cover and simmer 15 minutes.

Yield: 10 servings

Serve as a side dish or on thickly sliced Italian bread for a delicious sandwich. A Far family favorite and loved by all!

"All that I am or hope to be, I owe to my Angel Mother."

~ Abraham Lincoln

Daddy's Roasted Peppers

4 bell peppers, sweet red, bell or
  mixed

Salt and pepper to taste
Olive oil

Rinse and dry peppers. Grill on all sides until charred and softened. Cool. Seed, core and slice peppers. Discard liquid. Place in a bowl. Sprinkle with salt and pepper. Drizzle with oil and toss to coat.

Yield: 4 to 6 servings

Traditionally, our father grilled peppers whenever he cooked out. They were served whole.

Mashed Sweet Potato Casserole

6 large sweet potatoes
½ cup orange juice
½ cup heavy cream
4 tablespoons unsalted butter,
  melted
¼ cup packed light brown sugar

½ teaspoon grated nutmeg
½ teaspoon cinnamon
⅛ teaspoon ground cardamom
2 teaspoons salt
1 teaspoon pepper

Scrub potatoes and pierce with a fork several times. Place on a non stick foil-lined baking sheet. Bake at 375 degrees 1 hour or until very soft. Cool completely. Scoop out pulp to an electric mixer bowl. Add orange juice, cream, butter, brown sugar, nutmeg, cinnamon, cardamom, salt and pepper. Mix until well combined. Transfer mixture to a baking dish. Bake at 350 degrees 25 minutes.

Yield: 6 to 8 servings

Sweet Potato Oven Fries

6 sweet potatoes, cut into French
    fry slices
¼ cup vegetable oil

1 teaspoon salt
½ teaspoon pepper

Combine potatoes, oil, salt and pepper. Toss to coat well. Spread in a single layer on a baking sheet. Bake at 400 degrees 20 to 25 minutes until crisp.

Yield: 8 to 10 servings

This can be prepared with white potatoes. Sweet potatoes are wonderful and a healthier substitute.

Sweet Potato Purée Laced with Bourbon

3 pounds sweet potatoes
4 tablespoons butter
¼ cup packed dark brown sugar
1 tablespoon cornstarch
1 teaspoon salt

¾ teaspoon cinnamon
½ teaspoon grated nutmeg
½ cup milk
⅓ cup bourbon

Place unpeeled potatoes in a large stockpot and cover with water. Bring to boil. Cook 20 to 25 minutes until tender. Cool slightly. Peel off skin and transfer to a large bowl. Mash using a potato masher, not a food processor. Add butter, brown sugar, cornstarch, salt, cinnamon and nutmeg. Mash until smooth. Stir in milk and bourbon. Spread mixture into a buttered 2-quart casserole dish. Dot with butter and sprinkle with brown sugar. (At this point, you may allow mixture to cool, cover and refrigerate or freeze.) Bake at 350 degrees 45 minutes or until lightly browned.

Yield: 8 to 10 servings

May top sweet potatoes with marshmallows instead of butter and brown sugar.

Maple Apple Sweets

4 to 5 medium sweet potatoes,
  cooked with skin on
4 to 5 medium apples, peeled and
  sliced

1 cup maple syrup
2-3 tablespoons butter

Cool, peel and slice sweet potatoes. Set aside. Combine apples, syrup and butter in a saucepan. Gently cook until apples are tender. Layer potatoes and apples in a buttered 3-quart casserole dish. Pour pan juices on top. Warm in the oven.

Yield: 6 to 8 servings

Sweet Potato Casserole

1 (29-ounce) can sweet potatoes
2 eggs
½ cup sugar
1 cup evaporated milk
½ teaspoon cinnamon
½ teaspoon ground cardamom

5 tablespoons butter, softened
1 cup crushed corn flakes
½ cup packed brown sugar
5 tablespoons butter, melted
½ cup chopped walnuts

Beat potatoes, eggs, sugar, milk, cinnamon, cardamom and butter until smooth. Spread mixture into a greased large quiche pan. Bake at 400 degrees 15 minutes. Combine corn flake crumbs, brown sugar, butter and walnuts. Spread over potatoes. Bake an additional 15 minutes.

Yield: 8 servings

Yukon Gold and Sweet Potato Mash

7 Yukon gold potatoes, peeled and
cut into pieces
3 sweet potatoes, peeled and
cut into pieces

1 stick butter
½ cup sour cream
Salt and pepper to taste

Place potatoes in a large stockpot and cover with water. Bring to boil. Reduce heat and cook until tender. Strain potatoes. Place in a bowl. Add butter, sour cream, salt and pepper. Whip until smooth.

Yield: 6 servings

Make this recipe in place of regular potatoes.

Tim's Grilled Potatoes

4 medium baking potatoes
4 medium Vidalia onions, skins
removed, sliced and halved

Olive oil
Salt, pepper, dried oregano and
parsley to taste

Slice each potato to ¼-inch thick slice while keeping intact. Place onion slices in between potato slices, starting and ending with potatoes. Onion slices need to be small size as potato slices to ensure even cooking. Place each potato on foil large enough to wrap potato. Drizzle with oil and sprinkle with salt, pepper, oregano and parsley. Wrap up each potato. Grill 15 minutes on each side. To serve, remove foil and place in a large serving bowl.

Yield: 4 to 6 servings

May substitute sweet potatoes for a delicious variation!

Elegant Baked Potatoes

4 medium potatoes
2 tablespoons butter, melted
½ teaspoon salt

1 tablespoon unseasoned fine dry bread crumbs
3 tablespoons butter, melted
1 tablespoon Parmesan cheese

Slice each potato crosswise at ⅛-inch intervals to within ¼-inch bottom. Arrange potatoes in a buttered pie plate. Drizzle with 2 tablespoons butter and sprinkle with salt. Bake at 425 degrees 30 minutes. Sprinkle with bread crumbs and drizzle with remaining butter. Bake an additional 20 minutes. Top with cheese and baste with butter. Bake 5 minutes more or until golden browned.

Yield: 4 servings

Traditional Scalloped Potatoes

3 tablespoons butter
2 tablespoons all-purpose flour
1½ teaspoons salt
⅛ teaspoon pepper

3 cups milk
6 medium potatoes, peeled and thinly sliced
2 medium onions, peeled and thinly sliced

Melt butter in a saucepan. Whisk in flour, salt and pepper. Gradually add milk. Whisk until sauce thickens. Place half the potatoes in a greased 2-quart casserole dish. Top with half the onions and half the sauce. Repeat layers. Cover and bake at 350 degrees 1 hour. Uncover and bake an additional 30 minutes.

Yield: 4 to 6 servings

Mommy's Pilaf

4-5 tablespoons butter
4 pieces dry thin spaghetti, broken
  into ½-inch pieces
1 tablespoon minced sweet red
  pepper

2 cups Uncle Ben's rice
5 cups chicken broth
Salt to taste
1 tablespoon minced parsley

Melt butter in a saucepan. Add spaghetti and red pepper. Cook and stir until browned. Add rice and stir until coated. Add broth and bring to boil. Season with salt. Top with parsley. Do not stir. Cover and cook 20 minutes until tender.

Yield: 6 servings

Kit's Thanksgiving Stuffing

2 (1-pound) packages regular
  pork sausage
1 (8-ounce) package sliced
  mushrooms
1½ cups diced onions
¾ cup diced carrots
1½ cups celery
3 garlic cloves, minced
1 (10-ounce) package frozen
  chopped spinach, thawed
  and drained

2 teaspoons dried rosemary
2 teaspoons poultry seasoning
1 teaspoon pepper
1 (15-ounce) package herbed dry
  bread stuffing
2 cups chicken broth
1 egg, lightly beaten

Cook sausage until browned. Add mushrooms, onions, carrots, celery and garlic. Cook 10 minutes, stirring frequently. Place mixture in a large bowl. Add spinach, rosemary, poultry seasoning, pepper, stuffing, broth and egg. Mix well. Pour mixture into a buttered 4-quart casserole dish. Cover and bake at 325 degrees 1 hour.

Yield: 10 to 12 servings

This may be made in advance and reheated in the oven.

Acorn Squash with Cranberry Pecan Filling

4 acorn squash
1 cup coarsely chopped cranberries
¾ cup chopped pecans
½ cup packed brown sugar

1 stick butter, melted
½ cup orange marmalade
½ teaspoon cinnamon

Cut squash in half lengthwise. Remove seeds and place cut sides down in a buttered baking sheet. Bake at 375 degrees 30 minutes. Combine cranberries, pecans, brown sugar, butter, marmalade and cinnamon. Turn squash cut sides up. Fill squash with cranberry mixture. Cover with foil. Bake at 350 degrees 45 minutes or until squash is tender.

Yield: 6 servings

As a substitute for the orange marmalade, we have used Rhubarb-Orange Conserve. This delicious conserve is made by the Trappist Monks of St. Joseph's Abbey in Spencer, Massachusetts. Their jellies, jams and conserves are the best!

Summertime Squash

1 tablespoon vegetable oil
1 teaspoon butter
2 small zucchini, cut into
    ¼-inch slices
2 small yellow squash, cut into
    ¼-inch slices

1 large sweet red pepper, cut into
    ¼-inch thick strips
2 garlic cloves, minced
¼ teaspoon salt
⅛ teaspoon pepper

Heat oil and butter in a large skillet. Sauté zucchini and squash until crisp-tender. Add red pepper, garlic, salt and pepper. Cook 3 minutes, stirring constantly.

Yield: 4 servings

Baked Acorn Squash

1 medium acorn squash, cut in
 half lengthwise
2 teaspoons butter
2 pears, peeled and diced

2 Granny Smith apples, peeled
 and diced
Juice of ½ lemon
½ teaspoon ground nutmeg
1 teaspoon cinnamon

Place squash skin side down on a baking sheet. Place 1 teaspoon butter in each half. Cover with foil and bake at 400 degrees 45 minutes or until soft. Remove from oven. Combine pears and apples with juice. Add nutmeg and cinnamon. Spoon mixture into squash halves. Cover with foil and return to oven. Bake 15 minutes more. Cut into quarters and serve warm.

Yield: 2 servings

As an alternative, our mother put a dot of butter, dash of cinnamon and nutmeg and a teaspoon of brown sugar in each half. She used to plan on 1 acorn squash cut in half for 2 people. Hence, 2 squash for 4 people. May even drop a marshmallow onto the top of above mixture!

Spinach and Bulgur Wheat

6 tablespoons butter
2 large onions, finely chopped
3½ cups water
¾ cup bulgur wheat

2½ teaspoons salt
1 pound spinach leaves, rinsed and
 well drained
⅛ teaspoon pepper

Melt butter in a saucepan. Sauté onions until browned. Set aside. Combine water, wheat and salt in a separate saucepan. Cover and cook over medium heat 15 minutes. Add spinach, onions and pepper to wheat mixture. Cover and simmer over low heat 15 minutes. Serve hot!

Yield: 6 servings

Creamed Spinach

2 cups chopped yellow onions
3 tablespoons unsalted butter
2 tablespoons all-purpose flour
⅛ teaspoon grated nutmeg
½ cup heavy cream
1 cup milk

3 (10-ounce) packages frozen
  chopped spinach, thawed and
  well drained
¼ cup grated Parmesan cheese
1½ teaspoons salt
¼ teaspoon black pepper
¼ cup Parmesan cheese
¼ cup grated Gruyère cheese

Sauté onions in butter about 12 minutes until tender. Add flour and nutmeg. Cook 2 minutes. Whisk in cream and milk until thickened. Add spinach, Parmesan cheese, salt and pepper. Mix well. Place spinach mixture in a baking dish. Sprinkle with Parmesan cheese. Top with Gruyère cheese. Bake at 425 degrees 20 minutes or until hot.

Yield: 8 servings

Fried Green Tomatoes

5 medium tomatoes, sliced thick
Salt and pepper to taste
2 eggs, beaten

½ cup bread crumbs
4 tablespoons butter

Sprinkle tomato slices with salt and pepper. Dip in egg. Lightly dredge in bread crumbs. Heat butter in a skillet. Fry tomatoes until browned on both sides. May top with peach chutney and a dollop of sour cream

Yield: 6 servings

A Charleston, South Carolina favorite and a summertime favorite of ours!

Stuffed Baked Tomatoes

8 medium tomatoes
Salt to taste
6 green onions, chopped
¼ cup olive oil
1 (10-ounce) package frozen
   chopped spinach, thawed and
   squeezed dry

⅓ cup chopped parsley
½ teaspoon dried basil
½ teaspoon dried thyme
6 tablespoons crumbled
   feta cheese

Slice tops off tomatoes. Scoop out the pulp, chop and reserve. Lightly salt inside of tomato. Invert on paper towels to drain. Sauté green onions, tomato pulp in oil 3 to 4 minutes. Add spinach, parsley, basil and thyme. Cook and stir over medium heat until liquid evaporates. Stir in 3 tablespoons cheese. Spoon spinach mixture into tomato shells. Place in a greased baking dish. Sprinkle with remaining cheese. The tomatoes may be refrigerated at this point until ready to heat. Bake at 375 degrees 10 to 15 minutes or until heated thoroughly. Do not let skins split open.

Yield: 8 servings

Fresh Corn and Tomato Salad

6 ears corn
2 tablespoons olive oil
1 tablespoon finely chopped garlic
½ cup packed julienne fresh basil
   leaves

1 tablespoon olive oil
12 cherry tomatoes, halved
2 tablespoons balsamic vinegar
Salt and pepper to taste

Cut corn kernels from cob. Heat oil in a large skillet. Sauté corn and garlic about 5 minutes until tender. Remove from heat. Add basil and mix well. Transfer mixture to a large bowl. Cool slightly, stirring occasionally. Add oil, tomatoes and vinegar. Mix gently. Sprinkle with salt and pepper. Cover and refrigerate until ready to serve.

Yield: 6 servings

Tabouleh
(Cracked Wheat Salad)

1½ cups fine or medium bulgur
   wheat
1 large bunch green onions,
   finely minced
1 small bunch mint, chopped
½ teaspoon pepper

1 large bunch flat leaf parsley, minced
4 tomatoes, chopped
½ cup olive oil
½ cup lemon juice
½ cup water
Salt to taste

Cover wheat with water and let soak 30 minutes. Drain excess water. Add onions, mint, pepper, parsley and tomatoes. Mix well. Just before serving, stir in oil, juice, water and salt.

Yield: 6 servings

Zucchini and Tomato

2½ pounds zucchini, cut into
   ½-inch pieces
1 pint grape tomatoes, halved
3 garlic cloves, thinly sliced

¼ cup chopped flat leaf parsley
5 tablespoons olive oil
Salt and pepper to taste

Combine zucchini, tomatoes, garlic, parsley and oil. Toss to coat. Sprinkle with salt and pepper. Spread mixture on a baking sheet. Roast at 450 degrees 25 minutes.

Yield: 6 servings

Mediterranean Zucchini

3 cups finely chopped zucchini
1 cup biscuit baking mix
½ medium onion, chopped
⅓ cup Parmesan cheese
2 tablespoons chopped parsley
½ teaspoon salt

½ teaspoon dried oregano
1 garlic clove, minced
½ cup vegetable oil
4 eggs, beaten
1 (8-ounce) container crumbled
  feta cheese

Combine zucchini, baking mix, onions, Parmesan cheese, parsley, salt, oregano, garlic, oil, eggs and feta cheese. Mix well. Spread mixture into a buttered 13 x 9 x 2-inch baking dish. Bake at 350 degrees 40 minutes. Cool slightly and cut into squares. Serve warm.

Yield: 10 to 12 servings

This recipe can be cut into 2-inch squares and served as an appetizer. It yields 48 squares. May bake and freeze squares. To serve, bake frozen squares at 350 degrees 15 minutes. A great way to use the zucchini from the garden!

Pink and Blue Pie

4 eggs
1⅓ cups half-and-half
1 teaspoon salt
Dash of pepper

¾ pound smoked bacon,
  cooked and crumbled
2 cups grated blue cheese or
  Jarlsberg cheese
1 (9-inch) unbaked pie shell

Blend eggs, half-and-half, salt, pepper and bacon. Mix well. Sprinkle cheese on the bottom of pie shell. Pour egg mixture on top. Bake at 350 degrees 1 hour or until center is set.

Yield: 8 servings

Mr. MacGregor's Garden with Goat Cheese

1 medium onion, cut into
   ½-inch slices
1 medium sweet red pepper, cut
   into ½-inch strips
1 medium yellow pepper, cut into
   ½-inch strips
4 tablespoons olive oil
3 garlic cloves, minced

½ eggplant, peeled and thinly
   sliced
Salt and pepper to taste
6 tomatoes, thinly sliced
2 large zucchini, thinly sliced
3 tablespoons chopped herbs
   (thyme, oregano, parsley)
8 ounces soft mild goat cheese

Sauté onions and peppers in 2 tablespoons oil until tender. Add garlic and sauté 1 minute. Spread mixture on the bottom of a 13 x 9 x 2-inch baking dish. Arrange eggplant on top. Sprinkle with salt and pepper. Layer alternating rows of tomatoes and zucchini, overlapping slightly. Sprinkle with herbs. Drizzle with 2 tablespoons oil and sprinkle with salt and pepper. Bake at 350 degrees 50 minutes until tender and lightly browned. Baste occasionally with pan juices. Top with cheese and bake an additional 5 minutes or until cheese melts.

Yield: 8 servings

A wonderful addition to any buffet!

Notes

_____

_____

_____

_____

_____

_____

_____

_____

_____

_____

_____

_____

_____

_____

_____

_____

Main Dishes

*"If you want to have a dinner, the White House
is the best place to do it. You can just say, "Tonight I want 75 people
for dinner." You don't have to worry about it. It happens."*

~ FORMER FIRST LADY NANCY REAGAN

Tenderloin with Roquefort Garlic Cream

6 (8-ounce) filet mignons
Salt and pepper to taste
½ head garlic
2 tablespoons vegetable oil

¾ cup heavy cream
¼ cup Roquefort cheese
3 tablespoons brandy
3 tablespoons dry vermouth

Sprinkle steak with salt and pepper. Place garlic on a small baking sheet. Drizzle with oil. Bake at 350 degrees 25 minutes. Cool and remove skin. Purée garlic with cream and cheese. Transfer cream to a skillet. Over low heat, stir in brandy and vermouth. Simmer until sauce thickens slightly. Grill steak to desired degree of doneness. Pour sauce over filets.

Yield: 6 servings

Asian Flank Steak

3 tablespoons gingerroot, peeled
   and minced
2 tablespoons minced jalapeño
   peppers
½ cup mint

4 garlic cloves, minced
½ cup lime juice
½ cup soy sauce
4 (½-pound) flank steaks
Mint sprigs for garnish

Combine ginger, jalapeño peppers, mint and garlic in a food processor. Pulse to combine and mince. Transfer to a 2-quart zip lock bag. Add juice and soy sauce. Lightly score meat and add to marinade. Marinate at least 8 hours or overnight. Grill steak to desired degree of doneness. Slice and serve. Garnish with mint.

Yield: 4 servings

Beef Curry on Rice

½ garlic clove, peeled and minced	1 pound round steak, cubed
4 cups sliced onions	1 beef bouillon cube
2 tablespoons vegetable oil	1 cup boiling water
1 tablespoon all-purpose flour	1 teaspoon curry powder
1 teaspoon salt	½ cup tomato juice
⅛ teaspoon pepper	1 cup cooked rice
2 tablespoons vegetable oil	

Sauté garlic and onions in 2 tablespoons oil until tender. Remove vegetables. Combine flour, salt, pepper and meat in a plastic bag. Toss to coat. Heat oil in skillet. Add meat and brown on all sides. Arrange onions and garlic on meat. Dissolve bouillon in water. Add to skillet. Stir in curry. Cover and simmer 1 hour, 15 minutes. Add tomato juice. Heat thoroughly and serve over a bed of rice.

Yield: 4 servings

Here is another recipe from Aunt Pat.

Firecracker London Broil

2 pounds London broil	2 medium plum tomatoes
½ teaspoon pepper	½ small onion
½ teaspoon salt	3 tablespoons balsamic vinegar
1 teaspoon sugar	¼ cup parsley
4-6 jalapeño peppers, stems removed	2 garlic cloves

Trim beef and cut into large pieces. Place in a zip-top plastic bag. Combine pepper, salt, sugar, jalapeño peppers, tomatoes, onion, vinegar, parsley and garlic in a food processor. Process until blended. Add to beef and toss to coat. Refrigerate 24 hours. Remove from marinade. Grill to desired degree of doneness. Slice beef and arrange on a platter.

Yield: 6 servings

Gingered Beef and Pineapple Stir-Fry

1 pound lean flank steak
1 tablespoon gingerroot, peeled and minced
2 teaspoons sugar
2 tablespoons low sodium soy sauce
2 tablespoons cooking sherry
3 garlic cloves, minced
2 teaspoons dark sesame seed oil
2 teaspoons cornstarch

1 tablespoon plus 1 teaspoon rice vinegar
2 cups cubed pineapple
1 cup 3-inch diagonally sliced green onions
1 cup thinly sliced mushrooms
¼ pound snow peas
1 cup 3-inch julienne cut sweet red pepper strips
6 cups cooked angel hair pasta

Trim fat from steak. Cut lengthwise with the grain into ¼-inch slices. Cut slices in half crosswise. Combine ginger, sugar, soy sauce, sherry and garlic in a zip-top plastic bag. Add steak and toss to coat. Refrigerate at least 2 hours, turning occasionally. Remove steak from bag and discard marinade. Spray a large skillet with cooking spray. Add oil and heat until hot. Add steak and cook 4 minutes. Whisk together cornstarch and vinegar. Add cornstarch, pineapples, onions, mushrooms, snow peas and peppers. Stir-fry 3 minutes or until vegetables are crisp-tender. Serve over pasta. Each serving should have 1 cup pasta and 1 cup steak mixture.

Yield: 6 servings

"All great change in America begins at the dinner table."
~ RONALD REAGAN

Grilled Tenderloin Steaks

¾ cup balsamic vinegar
1½ tablespoons sugar
2 (10-ounce) tenderloin steaks

Salt and pepper to taste
4 ounces crumbled goat cheese,
    blue or Gorgonzola cheese

Cook vinegar and sugar until it reaches a syrupy consistency. Set aside and keep warm. Sprinkle steaks with salt and pepper. Grill streaks to desired degree of doneness. Place steaks on two dinner plates. Drizzle with syrup and top with cheese.

Yield: 2 servings

Grilled Rib-Eye
with Pistachio Butter

2 sticks butter, softened
2 tablespoons pistachios, toasted
    and minced
Juice of 2 lemons
1 tablespoon chopped parsley

1 tablespoon chopped chives
1 shallot, minced
Kosher salt and pepper to taste
4 (12-ounce) rib-eye steaks,
    1½-inches thick

Combine butter, pistachios, juice, parsley, chives and shallot in a food processor. Process until smooth. Stir in salt and pepper. Scoop butter onto plastic wrap. Roll into a thick log. Refrigerate until chilled. Sprinkle steaks liberally with salt and pepper. Let stand 1 hour. Grill steak to desired degree of doneness. To serve, slice butter into ¼-inch pieces and place on hot steaks. Allow butter to melt.

Yield: 4 to 6 servings

Honey Dijon Beef Stir-Fry

3 cups frozen French fried potatoes
1 pound beef round tip steaks, cut
⅛-inch to ¼-inch thick
1 red onion, cut lengthwise into
thin wedges

1 sweet red or bell pepper,
julienne cut
⅓ cup honey-Dijon barbecue
sauce

Prepare potatoes according to package directions. Keep warm. Stack beef steaks and cut lengthwise in half and then crosswise into 1-inch strips. Spray a large skillet with cooking spray and heat until hot. Stir-fry half of beef at a time 1 minute or until no longer pink. Remove from skillet. Stir-fry remaining beef, and then remove. Add onions and peppers. Stir-fry 5 minutes or until crisp-tender. Return beef to skillet. Add barbecue sauce and heat thoroughly. Spoon beef mixture over potatoes. Serve immediately.

Yield: 4 servings

Armenian Hamburgers

1 pound ground sirloin
½ cup fine bulgur wheat
1 small onion, finely chopped
¼ cup chopped flat leaf parsley
1 tomato, diced

2 tablespoons finely minced
mint or 1 teaspoon dried
1 teaspoon salt
½ teaspoon pepper

Combine sirloin, wheat, onions, parsley, tomatoes, mint, salt and pepper. Shape mixture into 6 medium size patties. Grill to desired degree of doneness.

Yield: 6 servings

Traditionally served with rice pilaf, Armenian cracker bread and tossed salad.

Kennebunkport Kabobs

MARINADE

⅓ cup olive oil
¼ cup balsamic vinegar
2 tablespoons soy sauce
1 teaspoon lemon juice
2 tablespoons Worcestershire sauce

2 garlic cloves, minced
1 tablespoon Dijon mustard
1 teaspoon chopped parsley
Salt and pepper to taste

Whisk together oil, vinegar, soy sauce, juice, Worcestershire sauce, garlic, mustard, parsley, salt and pepper.

SKEWERED KABOBS

1-1½ pounds cubed beef
1 sweet red pepper, cut into pieces
1 yellow pepper, cut into pieces

1 large Vidalia onion, cut into pieces
1 pint cherry tomatoes
1 pint mushrooms

Place beef in a zip-top plastic bag. Pour marinade over beef and toss to coat. Refrigerate 1 hour. Pierce beef and vegetables onto skewers in an alternating fashion. Brush kabobs with extra marinade. Grill until desired degree of doneness, turning skewers occasionally.

Yield: 4 servings

"It's fun to feed a man…when you do it right!"
~ BETTY CROCKER

Barbeque Beef Brisket

4-6 pound whole beef brisket
1 (6-ounce) bottle liquid smoke
Salt, garlic and celery salt
2 onions, chopped

Worcestershire sauce
1 (6 to 12-ounce) bottle barbecue
sauce

Trim fat off brisket. Pour liquid smoke over brisket. Liberally sprinkle with salt, garlic salt and celery salt. Top with onions. Cover and refrigerate overnight. Before cooking, pour off liquid smoke. Cover with Worcestershire sauce. Cover with foil and bake at 275 degrees 5 to 6 hours. Uncover and top with barbecue sauce. Bake an additional hour.

Yield: 10 to 12 servings

Be sure to look for our homemade barbecue sauce recipe. It really does the trick!

Barbecue Beef and Beans

1 pound ground sirloin beef
1 pound bacon, chopped
1 onion, chopped
½ cup barbecue sauce
¾ teaspoon pepper
1 teaspoon chili powder
4 teaspoons molasses

¼ cup prepared mustard
½ cup ketchup
1 teaspoon salt
2 (16-ounce) cans butter beans
2 (16-ounce) cans red kidney
beans, drained
2 (16-ounce) cans pork and beans

Brown beef, bacon and onions. Drain excess fat. Stir in barbecue sauce, pepper, chili powder, molasses, mustard, ketchup and salt. Stir thoroughly. Add all beans and mix well. Transfer to a bean pot. Bake at 350 degrees 1 hour.

Yield: 20 to 24 servings

Beef and Green Onion Roll-Ups

1 tablespoon canola oil
1 sweet red pepper, julienne
1 tablespoon soy sauce
1 pound sirloin steaks, cut into
   8 slices
Salt and pepper to taste
1 tablespoon canola oil

4 green onions, trimmed, thinly
   sliced lengthwise and cut into
   2-inch pieces
2 tablespoons water
2 tablespoons soy sauce
2 tablespoons rice vinegar
2 teaspoons sugar

Heat 1 tablespoon oil in a large skillet over medium-high heat. Add peppers and cook until pepper blisters. Add soy sauce. Transfer to a plate. Wipe skillet clean. Pound steak between plastic wrap to ⅛-inch thick pieces. Sprinkle with salt and pepper. Divide pepper strips and green onions among steak slices. Roll steak up tightly into bundles. Secure each roll with a toothpick. Heat oil in skillet over medium heat. Working in two batches, sear bundles until browned on all sides, 3 to 4 minutes. Transfer to a plate and keep warm. Wipe out skillet. Add water, soy sauce, vinegar and sugar. Cook over medium heat, stirring until reduced and syrupy. Remove toothpicks. Drizzle sauce over beef rolls.

Yield: 4 servings

Beef Taco Salad

1¼ pounds ground sirloin
1½ tablespoons chili powder
½ teaspoon ground cumin
½ teaspoon salt
¼ teaspoon pepper

1¼ cups salsa
Mixed greens
Chopped tomatoes, olives and
   green onions
1 cup shredded Cheddar cheese

Brown beef until no longer pink. Add chili powder, cumin, salt and pepper. Stir in salsa. Heat thoroughly. Arrange lettuce on dinner plates. Place a spoonful of beef in the center. Garnish with tomatoes, olives and green onions. Sprinkle with cheese.

Yield: 4 servings

Sun-Dried Tomato Burgers

1 pound ground sirloin
3 tablespoons minced parsley
⅓ cup sun-dried tomatoes, hydrated
  and chopped

¼ cup minced Vidalia onions
¼ teaspoon pepper
3 tablespoons teriyaki sauce
1 teaspoon Worcestershire sauce

Combine, sirloin, parsley, tomatoes, onions, pepper, teriyaki sauce and Worcestershire sauce. Mix well. Shape mixture into 5 patties. Cook to desired degree of doneness.

Yield: 5 servings

Everyone raves about these burgers!

Meatloaf

1 (3-ounce) can chopped
  mushrooms
Milk
1 egg, slightly beaten
1½ teaspoons Worcestershire sauce
1 teaspoon salt

½ teaspoon dry mustard
Dash of pepper
1½ cups bread crumbs
1½ pounds lean ground beef
¼ cup ketchup
2 tablespoons honey

Drain mushrooms, reserving liquid. Add enough milk to mushroom liquid to equal ½ cup. Combine reserved liquid, egg, Worcestershire sauce, salt, mustard, pepper and bread crumbs. Stir in beef and mushrooms. Mix well. Shape mixture into a loaf. Place in a 13 x 9 x 2-inch baking dish. Whisk together ketchup and honey. Spread over loaf. Bake at 350 degrees 1 hour.

Yield: 6 servings

Instead of 1 large loaf, you may make 6 to 8 smaller loaves using the same baking dish.

Daddy's Burger

1 pound ground sirloin
1 small onion, finely minced or
    ½ cup finely chopped green
    onions

1 tomato, diced
½ cup minced flat leaf parsley
1 teaspoon salt
½ teaspoon pepper

Combine sirloin, onions, tomatoes, parsley, salt and pepper. Mix well. Shape mixture into 6 patties. Grill to desired degree doneness.

Yield: 6 servings

A summer family favorite.

Stuffed Tomatoes and Peppers

2 medium zucchini squash,
    cut in half
2 medium summer squash,
    cut in half
4 medium tomatoes
4 Italian peppers

1 pound ground sirloin
½ cup fine bulgur wheat
1 medium onion, chopped
1 teaspoon salt
½ teaspoon pepper
2 (8-ounce) cans tomato sauce

Trim edges of squash. Scoop out squash leaving 1-inch pulp on the bottom, reserving pulp in a bowl. Set aside. Core the tomatoes. Scoop out the pulp and reserve in a bowl. Hollow out peppers, discarding core and seeds. Combine sirloin, wheat, onions, tomato pulp, salt and pepper. Mix well. Carefully stuff zucchini, squash, tomatoes and peppers with the meat mixture. Place vegetables in a covered roasting pan. Add tomato sauce to pan and enough water to cover halfway up vegetables. Chop reserved squash pulp. Stir into tomato sauce. Bake at 350 degrees 1 hour or until cooked.

Yield: 4 to 6 servings

Our mother always made this in the summer and early fall when vegetables from our local farmers are plentiful.

Swedish Meatballs

MEATBALLS

2 tablespoons chopped onions
5 tablespoons butter
½ cup half-and-half
½ cup bread crumbs
1½ pounds ground beef chuck
½ pound ground pork

2 eggs, slightly beaten
2 teaspoons salt
¼ teaspoon pepper
½ teaspoon ground allspice
2 dashes ground cloves

Sauté onions in butter until golden browned. Transfer to a bowl. Add half-and-half, bread crumbs, beef, pork, eggs, salt, pepper, allspice and cloves. Mix well. Shape mixture into small balls. Melt butter in a skillet. Cook meatballs until golden browned. Remove to a plate.

SAUCE

2 tablespoons all-purpose flour
1 cup heavy cream
1 cup water

½ teaspoon salt
Dash of pepper
½ teaspoon Gravy Master seasoning

Remove all but 2 tablespoons of drippings from skillet. Whisk in flour until smooth. Gradually stir in cream and water. Bring to boil. Reduce heat and add salt, pepper and gravy seasoning. Place meatballs in sauce and heat thoroughly.

Yield: 10 servings

This recipe is from an old family friend. It is great for a buffet.

Timberline Pie

1 tablespoon butter
½ cup diced onion
¼ cup quartered baby Bella
   mushrooms
½ cup diced carrots
½ cup all-purpose flour
½ teaspoon salt

¼ teaspoon pepper
1 pound beef stew meat, cubed
1 tablespoon butter
2 garlic cloves, minced
1 (14½-ounce) can beef broth
1 tablespoon tomato paste
4 cups hot mashed potatoes

Melt butter in a large skillet. Sauté onions, mushrooms and carrots 5 minutes until tender. Remove from skillet and set aside. Combine flour, salt and pepper in a zip-top plastic bag. Add beef and toss to coat. Melt butter in skillet and sauté garlic 10 seconds. Add beef and cook until browned. Remove to a plate. Add broth and scrape to deglaze skillet. Bring to boil and cook 5 minutes to reduce liquid by half. Stir in tomato paste and bring to boil. Return vegetables and beef to skillet. Cover and cook 15 minutes. Uncover and cook 15 more minutes. Place hot meat mixture in a deep dish 9-inch pie pan. Top with hot mashed potatoes, forming peaks. Broil 5 minutes until potato peaks are golden browned.

Yield: 6 servings

Aunt Lizzie's Pork Tenderloin

½ cup soy sauce
½ cup packed brown sugar
2 tablespoons vegetable oil
1 tablespoon toasted sesame seeds

1½ teaspoons grated ginger
6 garlic cloves, minced
2 (12 to 16-ounce) pork
   tenderloins

Combine soy sauce, brown sugar, oil, sesame seeds, ginger and garlic. Place tenderloins in a zip-top plastic bag. Pour marinade over meat. Refrigerate overnight. Remove meat and wrap in foil. Bring marinade to boil in a saucepan. Bake meat at 350 degrees 35 to 40 minutes. Serve with marinade.

Yield: 8 servings

Commander Willie's Colorado Casserole

½ pound bacon, cut into pieces
1 pound chopped sirloin
1 large onion, chopped
1 (16-ounce) can kidney beans, undrained

1 (16-ounce) can lima beans
1 (28-ounce) can pork and beans
½ cup ketchup
2 tablespoons vinegar
¼ cup packed brown sugar

Cook bacon until crisp. Remove from pan and pour off drippings. Brown sirloin and onions. Stir in bacon. Add kidney beans, lima beans and pork and beans. Stir in ketchup, vinegar and brown sugar. Transfer mixture in a bean pot. Bake at 350 degrees 1 hour.

Yield: 6 to 8 servings

Bourbon Marinated Pork Tenderloin

¾ cup soy sauce
½ cup bourbon
¼ cup Worcestershire sauce
¼ cup water
¼ cup canola oil
4 garlic cloves, minced

3 tablespoons packed brown sugar
1 tablespoon pepper
1 teaspoon white pepper
½ teaspoon ground ginger
2½ pounds whole pork tenderloin
1 teaspoon salt

Combine soy sauce, bourbon, Worcestershire sauce, water, oil, garlic, brown sugar, pepper, white pepper and ginger. Place tenderloin in a zip-top plastic bag. Add marinade and refrigerate at least 12 hours. Remove meat from marinade. Discard marinade. Sprinkle with salt. Grill meat, turning occasionally, 25 to 30 minutes or until meat thermometer reaches 155 degrees.

Yield: 10 servings

This is a favorite of Kathy's husband as he loves his bourbon!

Grilled Pork Tenderloin

2 whole pork tenderloins	2 tablespoons sesame oil
¼ cup grated ginger	2 garlic cloves, minced
2 tablespoons soy sauce	2 cups chicken broth

Combine tenderloins, ginger, soy sauce, oil, garlic and broth in a zip-top plastic bag. Refrigerate 2 to 24 hours. Remove meat and discard marinade. Grill tenderloins 15 to 20 minutes, turning occasionally, until thermometer reaches 155 degrees.

Yield: 6 servings

Maple Mustard Glazed Pork Roast

⅔ cup maple syrup	1 (2 to 3-pound) boneless pork loin roast
3 tablespoons Dijon mustard	1 pound carrots, peeled and quartered lengthwise
2 tablespoons cider vinegar	4-6 medium red potatoes, cleaned and halved
2 tablespoons soy sauce	
Salt and pepper to taste	

Combine syrup, mustard, vinegar, soy sauce, salt and pepper. Spread evenly over roast. Place in a shallow pan. Arrange carrots and potatoes in pan. Roast at 350 degrees 1 hour to 1 hour, 15 minutes or until thermometer reaches 155 to 160 degrees. Slice roast and serve with vegetables.

Yield: 6 servings

Other favorite vegetables can be substituted such as Brussels sprouts, winter squash wedges and sweet potatoes.

Peppered Pork Roast with Cherry Salsa

PORK

2 tablespoons pepper
2 teaspoons garlic salt

1 (3-pound) pork loin roast

Rub pepper and garlic salt onto pork roast. Place pork in a shallow pan. Roast at 350 degrees 1 hour or until thermometer reaches 155 to 160 degrees. Let roast stand 10 minutes before slicing. Serve with Cherry Salsa.

CHERRY SALSA

⅓ cup chopped onions
⅓ cup chopped bell peppers
⅓ cup chopped green chilies
⅓ cup chopped dried cherries

⅓ cup Trappist cherry jam
1½ tablespoons vinegar
1½ tablespoons chopped cilantro

Combine onions, peppers, chilies, cherries, jam, vinegar and cilantro. Mix well. Cover and refrigerate several hours or overnight.

Yield: 6 to 8 servings

Pork Chops with Orange and Marsala

2 tablespoons olive oil
4 pork loin chops, 1-inch thick
Salt and pepper to taste
½ cup Marsala

½ cup orange juice
½ teaspoon orange zest
Orange peel strips for garnish

Heat oil in a skillet. Brown chops on both sides about 10 minutes. Sprinkle with salt and pepper. Reduce heat to medium-low heat, cook another 15 minutes. Transfer to plate and keep warm. Add Marsala to skillet and cook 2 minutes until reduced and slightly thickened. Add juice and simmer. Return chops to skillet. Top with zest and cook 2 minutes basting with pan juices. Garnish with orange strips.

Yield: 4 servings

Grilled Maple Chipotle Pork Chops

½ cup barbecue sauce
½ cup maple syrup
2 chipotle peppers in sauce,
    seeded and minced

1 teaspoon sauce from chipotle
    peppers
6 thick bone-in pork chops
1 teaspoon salt
1 teaspoon pepper

Sprinkle pork chops with salt and pepper. Whisk together the barbecue, syrup, chipotle peppers and sauce. Place chops on a hot grill. Cover with grill lid and cook 20 minutes, turning once. Baste with half the barbecue sauce last 5 minutes of cooking. Serve with remaining sauce.

Yield: 6 servings

Chipotle peppers in adobo sauce may be found in the ethnic section of your supermarket.

Pork Chops with Rhubarb Stuffing

4 thick pork chops
Salt and pepper to taste
1 tablespoon vegetable oil
2½-3 cups soft bread crumbs

3 cups rhubarb, cut into
  1-inch pieces
½ cup all-purpose flour
1 teaspoon cinnamon
½ cup packed brown sugar

Sprinkle pork chops with salt and pepper. Brown chops in hot oil. Remove to a plate. Combine ¼ cup drippings with bread crumbs. Reserve ½ cup bread crumbs. Spread remaining bread crumbs in a 13 x 9 x 2-inch baking dish. Combine rhubarb, flour, cinnamon and brown sugar. Spoon half rhubarb mixture over bread crumbs. Place chops on top. Spoon remaining rhubarb mixture over chops. Cover with foil. Bake at 350 degrees 40 minutes. Remove foil and sprinkle with reserved bread crumbs. Bake another 10 to 15 minutes.

Yield: 4 servings

Easter Ham with Mustard Glaze

4 tablespoons unsalted butter
¼ cup packed brown sugar
⅓ cup Dijon mustard

1½ cups dry sherry
7-8 pound scored whole ham

Melt butter in a saucepan. Stir in brown sugar, mustard and sherry until smooth. Gently pour over ham. Bake at 325 degrees until cooked through. Baste with glaze.

Yield: 8 to 10 servings

This was served at memorable Easter dinners on our mother's wicker sun porch.

Spicy Pork Sandwiches

1 large onion, thinly sliced
2 pound boneless pork
   shoulder roast
1 tablespoon hot paprika
2 (14½-ounce) cans chunky
   chili-style tomatoes

1 (4½-ounce) can diced green chili
   peppers
2 teaspoons dried oregano, crushed
1 teaspoon pepper
¼ teaspoon salt
8 (6-inch) French style rolls, split
   and toasted

Arrange onions in the bottom of a 4-quart casserole dish. Sprinkle roast with paprika. Place roast over onions. Combine tomatoes, chili peppers, oregano, pepper and salt. Pour mixture over roast. Cover and bake at 325 degrees 2 hours, 15 minutes to 3 hours until roast is tender. Transfer roast to a cutting board. Shred pork with two forks. Skim fat from pan juices. Return meat to dish and mix well. Heat thoroughly. Spoon mixture onto rolls.

Yield: 8 servings

Peach Glazed Smoked Ham

7 pound half fully cooked, smoked
   bone-in ham
½ cup peach jam

3 tablespoons Dijon mustard
½ teaspoon ground ginger
Rosemary sprigs for garnish

Score ham, just through to meat into ¾-inch diamonds. Place on a rack in a roasting pan. Combine jam, mustard and ginger. Spread glaze over ham. Bake at 325 degrees until cooked through. Top with rosemary sprigs.

Yield: 8 to 10 servings

Georgia On My Mind Chicken

⅔ cup peach preserves
2 tablespoons chopped ginger
2 garlic cloves
2 tablespoons soy sauce
1 tablespoon English Breakfast Tea
　leaves

¼ teaspoon crushed red pepper
4 chicken legs
4 chicken thighs
4 chicken drumsticks
1½ teaspoons vegetable oil
Salt and pepper to taste

Combine preserves, ginger, garlic, soy sauce and tea leaves in a blender. Purée until smooth, scraping down sides. Stir in red pepper. Set aside. Brush chicken parts with oil. Brown chicken parts in a large oven-safe skillet 6 to 8 minutes. Drain off fat. Sprinkle with salt and pepper. Turn chicken and brown other side. Pour preserve mixture over chicken. Bake at 350 degrees 40 minutes. Baste occasionally with glaze.

Yield: 4 to 6 servings

Oven Crusted Baked Chicken

4 boneless skinless chicken
　breast halves
½ cup mayonnaise
¼ cup grated Parmesan cheese

¼ teaspoon pepper
1 tablespoon minced parsley
4 teaspoons Italian bread crumbs

Arrange chicken in a baking dish. Combine mayonnaise, Parmesan cheese, pepper and parsley. Spread mixture over each chicken breast. Sprinkle each with 1 teaspoon bread crumbs. Bake at 425 degrees 25 minutes.

Yield: 4 servings

Cranberry Harvest Chicken

4 boneless skinless chicken
   breast halves
¼ cup all-purpose flour
¼ cup vegetable oil
1 tablespoon minced shallots

½ cup chopped fresh cranberries
½ cup chicken broth
¼ cup white wine
1 tablespoon sugar
¼ cup apple cider

Dredge chicken in flour, shaking off excess. Heat oil over medium-high heat. Sauté chicken 7 to 9 minutes per side until golden browned. Transfer chicken to a serving platter and keep warm. Add cranberries and shallots to pan. Cook 2 minutes. Add broth and wine. Bring to low boil. Cook and stir until reduced by half. Stir in sugar and cider and reduce by half. Return chicken to pan and baste with sauce until thoroughly heated.

Yield: 4 servings

Apricots and Bows

1 (10-ounce) package farfalle pasta
1 rotisserie chicken, meat removed
1½ cups half-and-half
2 tablespoons butter

⅓ cup chopped green onions
1 (17-ounce) can apricot halves,
   drained and quartered
Salt and pepper to taste

Cook farfalle according to package directions. Place chicken in a large skillet. Stir in half-and-half and simmer 4 minutes. Add green onions and apricots. Simmer 2 to 3 minutes. Pour chicken mixture over pasta. Serve immediately.

Yield: 4 servings

Lovely for a ladies luncheon or an Easter buffet.

Banff Springs Chicken Breast with Orange Sauce

4 boneless, skinless chicken
   breast halves
Salt, pepper and ground coriander
   to taste
2 tablespoons olive oil
¼ cup diced carrots
¼ cup diced celery
¼ cup diced red onions

1 garlic clove, crushed and
   chopped
½ cup orange juice
½ cup white wine
2 cups chicken broth
4 saffron threads
2 tablespoons unsalted butter
2 teaspoons chopped cilantro

Sprinkle chicken with salt, pepper and coriander. Heat oil in an oven safe saucepan. Brown chicken on all sides until golden browned. Bake at 325 degrees 30 minutes until cooked through. Remove chicken and keep warm in the oven. Sauté carrots, celery, onions and garlic in saucepan. Add juice and wine. Deglaze the pan until liquid is reduced to one-third. Add broth and saffron. Simmer until reduced by half. Whisk in butter. Sprinkle with salt, pepper and cilantro. Slice each chicken breast into fourths. Arrange on four plates. Spoon sauce over chicken. Garnish with cilantro.

Yield: 4 servings

Chicken in Maple Sauce

1 egg, beaten
¼ cup milk
3 pounds boneless, skinless
    chicken breast halves
¾ cup bread crumbs

5 tablespoons vegetable oil
1 cup half-and-half
1 cup milk
½ cup maple syrup

Whisk together egg and milk. Dip chicken in mixture. Roll in bread crumbs and arrange in an oiled 13 x 9 x 2-inch baking dish. In a separate bowl, blend half-and-half, milk and syrup. Pour over chicken. Bake at 350 degrees 1 hour, 30 minutes, turning chicken every 30 minutes.

Yield: 6 to 8 servings

Chicken Curry

2 tablespoons olive oil
2 boneless, skinless chicken breast
    halves, split
Salt and pepper to taste
1 large onion, diced
1 tablespoon minced garlic

1 tablespoon grated ginger
1 tablespoon curry powder
1½ teaspoons ground garam masala
    (optional)
½ cup canned crushed tomatoes
¾ cup chicken broth

Heat oil in a skillet. Sprinkle chicken with salt and pepper. Brown chicken on both sides. Remove chicken and set aside. Reduce heat to medium. Sauté onions 2 minutes. Add garlic and cook until golden browned. Stir in ginger, curry and garam masala. Cook and stir 1 to 2 minutes. Add tomatoes and broth. Return chicken. Bring to boil. Cover and simmer 15 minutes, turning once.

Yield: 2 servings

Chicken Croquettes

SAUCE

3 tablespoons vegetable oil
½ cup all-purpose flour
½ teaspoon salt

Pepper to taste
1 cup milk

Heat oil in a saucepan. Whisk in flour. Stir in salt and pepper. Gradually blend in milk. Cook over medium heat 1 minute or until sauce thickens. Set aside.

CHICKEN

2 cups finely chopped cooked
    chicken
¾ teaspoon salt
½ teaspoon celery salt
Pepper to taste
1 teaspoon finely chopped onions

1 tablespoon chopped parsley
1 cup dry bread crumbs
1 egg, beaten
2 tablespoons water
Vegetable oil

Combine chicken, salt, celery salt, pepper, onions and parsley. Add the prepared sauce. Mix well and refrigerate several hours. Shape mixture into 10 balls. Roll in bread crumbs. Dip in the egg then water. Heat oil in a skillet. Fry each croquette 2 minutes or until golden browned. Drain on paper towels.

Yield: 4 servings

Utilize leftover chicken by making this recipe.

Chicken Gorgonzola

1 tablespoon olive oil
4 boneless, skinless chicken breast
 halves
Salt and pepper to taste
½ cup black olives, thinly sliced

1 (8-ounce) jar roasted red peppers,
 cut into strips
4 tablespoons butter
½ cup whipping cream
4 ounces crumbled Gorgonzola
 cheese

Heat oil in a large skillet. Sprinkle chicken with salt and pepper. Brown chicken on all sides and cook through. Add olives and peppers. Cook until heated. Remove mixture to a plate and keep warm in the oven. Melt butter in a saucepan. When butter foams, add cream. Bring to boil. Stir in cheese and reduce heat. Cook 3 to 4 minutes until sauce thickens. Arrange chicken and pepper mixture on four plates. Pour sauce over chicken and serve.

Yield: 4 servings

Chicken Pomodoro

1 pound package boneless
 chicken cutlets
Salt and pepper to taste
½ cup all-purpose flour
2 tablespoons vegetable oil
¼ cup vodka

½ cup chicken broth
2 tablespoons lemon juice
½ cup chopped tomatoes
2 tablespoons heavy cream
⅓ cup minced green onions

Sprinkle chicken with salt and pepper. Dust with flour, shaking off excess. Sauté chicken in oil until golden browned. Transfer to a warm plate. Remove drippings from pan. Add vodka and cook until reduced by half. Add broth and juice. Cook 2 minutes. Return chicken to skillet. Add tomatoes and cream. Cook 3 minutes. Garnish with green onions.

Yield: 4 servings

Chicken Piccata

1 pound package boneless
chicken cutlets
Salt and pepper to taste
¼ cup all-purpose flour
2 tablespoons vegetable oil
¼ cup white wine
1 teaspoon minced garlic

½ cup chicken broth
2 tablespoons lemon juice
1 tablespoon capers, drained
2 tablespoons unsalted butter
Lemon slices
Chopped parsley for garnish

Sprinkle chicken with salt and pepper. Dust with flour, shaking off excess. Sauté chicken in oil until golden browned on both sides. Transfer to a warm plate. Remove drippings from pan. Deglaze the pan with wine and garlic. Cook 2 minutes or until garlic is lightly browned and liquid is almost evaporated. Add broth, juice and capers. Return chicken to pan. Stir in butter and lemon slices. Garnish with parsley.

Yield: 4 servings

Mediterranean Chicken

4 boneless, skinless chicken
breast halves
Salt and pepper to taste
3 large shallots, chopped
2 teaspoons dried oregano
2 tablespoons olive oil

1 (14½-ounce) can undrained
diced tomatoes
1 (14½-ounce) can chicken broth
1 cup crumbled feta cheese
⅓ cup chopped kalamata olives

Sprinkle chicken with salt and pepper. Sauté shallots and oregano in oil 5 minutes. Add chicken and sauté 9 minutes per side. Stir in tomatoes and broth. Bring to boil. Reduce heat and simmer 10 minutes, stirring occasionally. Using a slotted spoon, remove chicken to a serving platter. Bring sauce to boil. Cook and stir 5 minutes until thickened. Reduce heat. Gently stir in cheese and olives. Return chicken. Simmer 5 minutes and serve.

Yield: 4 servings

Spicy Chicken and Peanuts

3 boneless, skinless chicken breast
  halves, rinsed and dried
1 tablespoon soy sauce
1 tablespoon cornstarch
2 tablespoons soy sauce
2 tablespoons cooking sherry
1 teaspoon sugar
1 teaspoon white vinegar

¼ cup chicken broth
¼ cup peanut oil
1 teaspoon crushed red pepper
½ cup sliced green onions
½ teaspoon ground ginger
½ cup peanuts
Hot cooked rice

Cut chicken into ½-inch pieces. Blend soy sauce and cornstarch. Add to chicken. Combine soy sauce, sherry, sugar, vinegar and broth in a small bowl. Set aside. Heat oil in a large skillet. Add red pepper and cook until blackened. Add chicken and cook until no longer pink. Remove to a plate. Add onions and ginger. Cook and stir 1 minute. Return chicken and cook 2 minutes. Pour in sherry mixture. Reduce heat and cook 1 minute, stirring constantly. Stir in peanuts. Serve over rice.

Yield: 4 servings

Citrus Ginger Grilled Chicken

4 boneless, skinless chicken
  breast halves
¼ cup plus 2 tablespoons
  orange juice
¼ cup soy sauce

1½ tablespoons rice vinegar
1 tablespoon grated ginger
1 tablespoon minced garlic
2 teaspoons crushed red pepper

Place chicken in a large zip-top plastic bag. Combine juice, soy sauce, vinegar, ginger, garlic and crushed red pepper. Pour marinade over chicken. Turn to coat. Refrigerate 30 minutes. Remove chicken and discard marinade. Grill chicken to desired degree of doneness.

Yield: 4 servings

Chicken Stuffed with Feta and Sun-Dried Tomatoes

½ cup sun-dried tomatoes, cut into strips
1 cup boiling water
½ cup finely chopped red onions
1 tablespoon olive oil
2 garlic cloves, minced
¼ cup pine nuts, lightly toasted

1 cup crumbled feta cheese
2 tablespoons Parmesan cheese
1 teaspoon dried marjoram
Salt and pepper to taste
4 boneless, skinless chicken breast halves
1 tablespoon olive oil

Combine sun-dried tomatoes with boiling water. Allow to soften. Drain. Sauté onions in oil until tender. Add garlic and cook 1 minute. Transfer to a bowl and let cool. Add tomatoes, nuts, feta cheese, Parmesan cheese and marjoram. Sprinkle with salt and pepper. Cut a pocket into each chicken breast. Fill with ¼ cup tomato mixture. Secure with toothpicks. Heat oil in a large skillet. Brown chicken on all sides. Transfer to a baking dish. Bake at 350 degrees 35 minutes.

Yield: 4 servings

Serve on a bed of fresh wilted spinach.

Grilled Lime Chicken

Juice of 2 limes
1 garlic clove, minced
¾ teaspoon chili powder
¼ teaspoon crushed red pepper

Pinch of salt and pepper
4 boneless skinless chicken breast halves

Combine lime juice, garlic, chili powder, red pepper, salt and pepper in a zip-top plastic bag. Add chicken and marinate 2 to 4 hours in refrigerator. Grill chicken until done.

Yield: 4 servings

Crispy Sun-Dried Tomato Chicken

4 boneless, skinless chicken
    breast halves
1 teaspoon pepper
½ teaspoon kosher salt
2 cups bread crumbs
½ cup oil-packed sun-dried
    tomatoes, drained and sliced

4 garlic cloves, peeled
½ cup all-purpose flour
2 eggs
2 tablespoons water
2 tablespoons olive oil

Pound chicken to ½-inch thickness. Sprinkle with salt and pepper. Combine bread crumbs, tomatoes and garlic in a food processor. Pulse mixture and transfer to shallow dish. Place flour in a separate dish. Whisk together eggs and water. Dredge chicken in flour and then dip in egg mixture to coat. Place in bread crumb mixture and pat on both sides to coat. Place on a plate. Heat oil in an ovenproof nonstick skillet. Sauté chicken on both sides until golden browned. Bake at 375 degrees 8 to 10 minutes.

BUTTER SAUCE
1 cup white wine
2 tablespoons crushed capers
2 tablespoons lemon juice
½ cup unsalted butter, thinly sliced

¼ cup oil-packed sun-dried
    tomatoes, drained and sliced
½ cup chopped parsley

Boil wine in a skillet until reduced by half. Add capers and juice. Boil 1 minute. Reduce heat to low. Whisk in butter 1 piece at a time until butter melts. Stir in tomatoes and parsley. Pour over chicken.

Yield: 4 servings

Honey Glazed Chicken Kabobs

CHICKEN KABOBS

4 large boneless, skinless chicken breast halves, cut into large pieces

1 large yellow squash, cut into large pieces

1 large zucchini, cut into large pieces

2 medium sweet red peppers, cut into large pieces

2 large onions, quartered

½ cup mushrooms, halved

Thread chicken and vegetables onto four 12-inch skewers. Grill 10 to 12 minutes or until desired degree of doneness. Brush with Honey Mustard Glaze. Grill 5 minutes more.

HONEY MUSTARD GLAZE

¾ cup honey

½ cup spicy mustard

2 tablespoons soy sauce

1 tablespoon cider vinegar

2 tablespoons cornstarch

¼ cup water

Combine honey, mustard, soy sauce and vinegar in a saucepan. Bring to boil. Whisk together cornstarch and water in a 1-cup measuring cup. Gradually whisk into honey mixture. Bring to boil. Boil, stirring constantly, 1 to 2 minutes until slightly thickened.

Yield: 4 servings

"We seldom report of having eaten too little."

~ Thomas Jefferson

Mexican Chicken Pie

3 boneless, skinless chicken
   breast halves, cubed
1 (14½-ounce) can chicken broth
½ cup diced celery
1 bell pepper, diced
1 medium onion, wedged
½ cup salsa

¾ cup frozen corn
2 tablespoons cornstarch
1 (8½-ounce) package
   cornbread mix
2 (4-ounce) cans diced green
   chilies, drained
1½ cups shredded Cheddar cheese

Combine chicken, broth, celery, peppers and onions in a stockpot. Bring to boil. Reduce heat and simmer 15 minutes. Add salsa and corn. Whisk in cornstarch and bring to boil. Simmer until mixture thickens. Prepare cornbread according to package directions. Pour chicken mixture into a 13 x 9 x 2-inch baking dish. Sprinkle with chilies and cheese. Spread cornbread batter on top. Bake at 425 degrees 20 minutes.

Yield: 6 servings

Wa's Chicken

Any amount chicken
Melted butter to coat chicken

Bread crumb stuffing to coat
   chicken

Dredge chicken in butter. Roll in stuffing. Place in a 13 x 9 x 2-inch baking dish. Cover with foil. Bake at 350 degrees 1 hour. Remove foil and bake until browned.

Yield: a few to many

Kathy's niece, Cricket, could not pronounce the name Julia as a little girl. Julia helped with the raising of Cricket and the other children. She retired after 43 years at Old Welbourne, their family home. Most of Middleburg now calls Julia "Wa" and her chicken is known throughout the world having been enjoyed by many foreign visitors.

Spicy Grilled Chicken with Pineapple Salsa

CHICKEN

1 head garlic, minced	1½ teaspoons ground thyme
2 tablespoons vegetable oil	1½ teaspoons dried oregano
3 pounds boneless, skinless chicken breast halves	¾ teaspoon cayenne pepper
	½ teaspoon salt
1½ teaspoons paprika	¼ teaspoon pepper

Combine garlic and oil. Add chicken and turn to coat all sides. In a separate bowl, combine paprika, thyme, oregano, cayenne, salt and pepper. Sprinkle over chicken and pat lightly. Grill over high heat 25 to 30 minutes or until cooked through. Serve immediately with pineapple salsa.

PINEAPPLE SALSA

½ pineapple, coarsely chopped	1 tablespoon chopped cilantro
1 large onion, chopped	1 teaspoon lime juice
1-2 jalapeño peppers, seeded and minced	1 teaspoon red wine vinegar
	⅛ teaspoon salt

Combine pineapple, onions, peppers, cilantro, juice, vinegar and salt. Mix well. Refrigerate at least 6 to 8 hours before serving.

Yield: 4 to 6 servings

Arroz Con Pollo

3 pounds chicken parts	3 teaspoons paprika
Salt to taste	¼ teaspoon saffron
6 tablespoons olive oil	2 cups short grain rice
2 bell peppers, chopped	3½ cups hot chicken broth
1 onion, chopped	½ cup dry white wine
2 garlic cloves, minced	Pepper to taste
2 tomatoes, peeled and chopped	1 tablespoon minced parsley
2 pimientos, chopped	

Sprinkle chicken parts with salt. Heat oil in a paella pan or a 15-inch ovenproof skillet. Fry chicken until golden browned. Remove to a platter. Sauté peppers, onions and garlic until tender. Stir in tomatoes and pimientos. Simmer 10 minutes. Add paprika and saffron. Stir in rice until well coated. Add hot broth, wine, salt and pepper. Boil, stirring constantly, 10 minutes until rice is no longer soupy. Arrange chicken over rice. Bake at 325 degrees 15 minutes. The liquid is absorbed but rice is al dente. Remove from oven and cover loosely with foil. Let stand 10 minutes. Sprinkle with parsley.

Yield: 8 servings

An ensalada and red wine are the only accompaniments necessary!

Lemon Basil Swordfish

2½ tablespoons lemon juice
2 tablespoons olive oil
2 garlic cloves, crushed
½ teaspoon lemon zest
2 tablespoons thinly sliced basil

2 teaspoons drained capers
Salt and pepper to taste
4 swordfish fillets
1 tablespoons thinly sliced basil

Blend juice, oil, garlic and zest. Add basil, capers, salt and pepper. Let vinaigrette stand 1 hour or longer. Sprinkle fillets with salt and pepper. Brush fillets with small amount of vinaigrette. Grill fillets 4 minutes per side. Remove to a serving plate. Whisk vinaigrette and pour over fillets. Top with basil.

Yield: 4 servings

Roasted Cod on Saffron Mashed Potatoes

2 pounds russet potatoes, peeled
and cut into 1½-inch pieces
½ cup whipping cream
¼ teaspoon crushed saffron
Salt and pepper to taste
4 (6-ounce) cod fillets

1½ teaspoons balsamic vinegar
3 tablespoons olive oil
1 cup arugula
½ cup mixed herbs
(basil, dill and tarragon)

Cook potatoes in boiling water 20 minutes until tender. Drain well. Return to pan and mash. Stir in cream and saffron. Sprinkle with salt and pepper. Cover to keep warm. Sprinkle cod with salt and pepper. Heat oil in an oven-proof skillet. Add cod and cook 2 minutes. Turn cod over. Place skillet in oven. Bake at 400 degrees 6 minutes until center is opaque. Combine vinegar and oil. Add arugula and herbs and toss to coat. Sprinkle with salt and pepper. Mound potatoes on four plates. Top with fish. Arrange salad around potatoes.

Yield: 4 servings

Haddock Valencia

3 pounds tomatoes, peeled and
   diced
¼ teaspoon saffron threads
2 small zucchini, thinly sliced
2 green onions, coarsely chopped

Salt and pepper to taste
2 tablespoons Parmesan cheese
1½ pound haddock fillet
¼ cup lemon juice

Combine tomatoes and saffron in a 3-quart saucepan. Simmer 20 minutes until juice evaporates and saffron breaks down. Add zucchini and green onions. Cook 2 minutes. Sprinkle with salt and pepper. Remove from heat. Stir in cheese. Place fillet in a buttered 13 x 9 x 2-inch baking dish. Sprinkle with juice. Top with vegetable mixture. Bake at 400 degrees 25 minutes.

Yield: 4 servings

Nancy's Baked Haddock with Lobster Sauce

¾ pound skinned haddock fillet
Salt and pepper to taste
2 tablespoons unsalted butter
1 tablespoon cornstarch
1 cup half-and-half

¼ teaspoon salt
⅛ teaspoon white pepper
3 tablespoons cooking sherry
¼ cup diced lobster meat

Place haddock in a buttered 13 x 9 x 2-inch baking dish. Sprinkle with salt and pepper. Set aside. Melt butter in a saucepan. Blend in cornstarch. Stir in half-and-half, salt and pepper until sauce thickens. Add sherry and lobster meat. Simmer 2 minutes. Pour mixture over haddock. Bake at 400 degrees 25 minutes.

Yield: 2 servings

To give this a kick, while making your sauce, add a dash of cayenne pepper. The fresh fish from Nickerson's Fish Market in Chatham, Massachusetts makes this dish hard to beat!

Grilled Swordfish with Pepper-Basil Salsa

SWORDFISH

4 (6-ounce) swordfish steaks	Salt and pepper to taste
1 tablespoon olive oil	

Brush steaks with oil on both sides. Grill over medium hot heat until just opaque. Sprinkle with salt and pepper. Top with salsa and serve hot.

PEPPER-BASIL SALSA

3 sweet red peppers	1 tablespoon red wine vinegar
2 garlic cloves, finely chopped	3 tablespoons olive oil
10 basil leaves, torn	Salt and pepper to taste

Grill, peel and seed the peppers. Finely dice peppers. In a bowl, combine peppers, garlic, basil, vinegar and oil. Stir in salt and pepper. Cover and let stand at room temperature 30 minutes to allow flavors to blend.

Yield: 4 servings

Baked Haddock with Stuffing

3 pounds haddock fillet	1½ cups prepared stuffing mix
1 (8-ounce) container sour cream	1 teaspoon dried marjoram
Salt and pepper to taste	1 teaspoon paprika

Place haddock on foil on a baking sheet. Spread sour cream over fish. Sprinkle with salt and pepper. Spread stuffing on top. Sprinkle with marjoram and paprika. Bake at 350 degrees 30 minutes or longer depending on thickness of fish.

Yield: 4 servings

Cape Cod Scrod

2 onions, sliced
1 sweet red pepper, cut into strips
2 yellow peppers, cut into strips
3 plum tomatoes, cut into thin
  wedges

½ cup olive oil
Dried oregano and chopped
  basil
4 (8-ounce) scrod fillets
Parmesan cheese for garnish

Sauté onions, peppers and tomatoes in oil until onions are clear. Add oregano and basil. Brush some oil on bottom side of fillet. Place in the bottom of a 13 x 9 x 2-inch baking dish. Divide vegetable mixture over each fillet. Top with Parmesan cheese. Bake at 400 degrees 20 minutes.

Yield: 4 servings

Lobster for Two

1 tablespoon unsalted butter
1 tablespoon minced garlic
1 teaspoon minced shallots
¼ cup Grand Marnier™
1 cup half-and-half

1¼ pounds cooked lobster
  meat, diced
Salt and pepper to taste
½ (9-ounce) package cheese
  tortellini, cooked al dente
Grated Romano cheese

Melt butter in a skillet. Sauté garlic and shallots 1 minute. Stir in Grand Marnier™. Add half-and-half and lobster meat. Cook and stir until slightly thickened. Sprinkle with salt and pepper. Pour mixture over tortellini. Sprinkle with cheese and serve immediately.

Yield: 2 servings

For an added flare, you may add fresh wilted spinach that has been drained well. Adds wonderful color and flavor.

Sconset's Surf and Turf

3-4 pound whole beef tenderloin, trimmed
2 cooked lobster tails
1 tablespoon butter, melted
1½ teaspoons lemon juice
6 slices bacon, slightly cooked

2 sticks butter
½ cup sliced green onions
2 garlic cloves, minced
1 cup dry white wine
2 teaspoons chopped tarragon

Butterfly cut tenderloin lengthwise to ½-inch of bottom. Remove lobster from shells and cut lengthwise. Place lobster end to end inside tenderloin pocket. Combine butter and juice. Drizzle over lobster. Close tenderloin around lobster and tie together with string at 1-inch intervals. Place on a rack in a shallow pan. Roast at 425 degrees 45 to 50 minutes for rare doneness. Lay bacon on top and roast 5 minutes more. Melt butter in a saucepan. Sauté onions and garlic until tender. Add wine and tarragon and heat thoroughly. Slice tenderloin and arrange on a platter. Pour wine sauce over meat.

Yield: 8 servings

Pan Seared Saffron Scallops

2 tablespoons olive oil
1 pound sea scallops
1 large tomato, peeled and chopped
1 tablespoon chopped shallots
1 cup white wine

1 pinch saffron
¼ cup heavy cream
3 tablespoons butter
Salt and pepper to taste
2 cups white rice, cooked
Chopped chives for garnish

Heat oil in a skillet. Sear scallops until golden browned. Add tomatoes and shallots. Sauté until hot. Add wine and saffron. Cook and stir until reduced by two-thirds. Add cream and reduce by one-half. Swirl in butter, salt and pepper and serve over bed of rice. Garnish with chives.

Yield: 2 to 3 servings

Nantucket Scallops and Spinach

24 large sea scallops
Olive oil
Salt and pepper to taste
1 teaspoon chopped garlic
3 tablespoons butter

1½ pounds fresh spinach, thinly
  sliced
3 tablespoons lemon juice
1 tablespoon water
5 tablespoons chilled butter

Brush both sides of scallops with oil. Sprinkle with salt and pepper. Arrange in a 13 x 9 x 2-inch baking dish. Bake at 400 degrees 10 minutes or until tender. Sauté garlic in butter 1 minute. Add spinach and cook 6 minutes until wilted. Add 1½ tablespoons juice, salt and pepper. Remove from heat and cover. Keep warm. Combine 1½ tablespoons juice and water in a saucepan. Bring to boil. Cook 2 minutes until liquid evaporates. Remove from heat. Whisk in 2 tablespoons butter. Place on low heat. Whisk in remaining butter 1 tablespoon at a time. Remove pan if drops of melted butter appear. If sauce breaks down, whisk in 2 tablespoons cold butter. Arrange wilted spinach on 4 plates. Top with scallops. Drizzle with lemon butter sauce.

Yield: 6 to 8 servings

"One cannot collect all the beautiful shells on the beach. One can collect only a few, and they are more beautiful if they are few."

~ ANNE MORROW LINDBERGH

Savory Scallops

1½ tablespoons olive oil
12 ounces large sea scallops, patted dry
½ cup dry white wine
3 tablespoons packed sun-dried tomatoes, drained and thinly sliced

¼ cup heavy cream
2 tablespoons butter, room temperature
2 teaspoons minced garlic
Salt and white pepper to taste

Heat a large skillet. Add oil when pan is hot, to prevent sticking. Add scallops and cook 2 minutes on both sides until browned and crusty. Do not overcrowd. Do in batches if necessary, turning once. Transfer and divide onto two plates. Keep warm. Add wine and tomatoes to skillet. Stir 2 minutes, scraping browned bits. Add cream and boil 2 minutes until reduced. Remove from heat. Add butter and garlic, whisking until melted. Stir in salt and pepper. Pour sauce over scallops and serve.

Yield: 2 servings

Scallops Brewster

2 pounds sea scallops
¼ cup lemon juice
½ cup dry white wine
4 tablespoons unsalted butter

1 cup crushed round buttery crackers
2 tablespoons minced parsley

Rinse scallops and dry very well. Arrange scallops in a buttered 13 x 9 x 2-inch baking dish. Pour juice and wine over scallops. Set aside. Melt butter and stir in cracker crumbs. Mix well. Spoon mixture over scallops. Sprinkle with parsley. Bake at 400 degrees 20 to 25 minutes.

Yield: 4 to 6 servings

This dish is a "10" thanks to the freshest scallops at Nickerson's Fish Market in Chatham on Cape Cod.

Scallops with Zesty Tartar Sauce

SCALLOPS

1 egg
2 tablespoons yogurt
½ teaspoon Tabasco sauce
¼ teaspoon salt
1 cup fine dry bread crumbs

⅓ cup fine yellow cornmeal
1⅓ pounds large sea scallops, patted dry
2 teaspoons unsalted butter, melted

Whisk together egg, yogurt, Tabasco and salt. Pour on a plate. Combine bread crumbs and cornmeal and spread on a plate. Dip scallops in egg mixture. Dredge in bread crumbs. Arrange in a greased 13 x 9 x 2-inch baking dish. Drizzle with butter. Bake at 475 degrees 8 minutes. Remove from the oven. Turn oven to broil. Place on top rack and broil until golden browned and cooked through. Serve with Zesty Tartar Sauce.

ZESTY TARTAR SAUCE

½ cup mayonnaise
½ teaspoon Tabasco sauce
2 tablespoons lime sections, peeled and finely chopped

2 tablespoons finely chopped green onions
1 tablespoon finely chopped cilantro
1 stalk celery, finely minced

Combine mayonnaise, Tabasco, lime sections, onions, cilantro and celery. Mix well. Refrigerate at least 1 hour.

Yield: 4 servings

"My life is like a stroll upon the beach,
as near the ocean's edge as I can go."
~ HENRY DAVID THOREAU, THE FISHER'S BOY

Seafood Bake

3 pounds seafood (scallops, shrimp, cooked lobster meat)
20 buttery round crackers, crushed
6 tablespoons butter
⅓ cup sherry
2 tablespoons lemon juice
1 teaspoon salt
½ teaspoon pepper
½ teaspoon onion powder
½ teaspoon garlic powder
Paprika to garnish
¼ cup minced flat leaf parsley

Peel and devein shrimp. Cut seafood into bite-size pieces. Arrange seafood in a 2-quart ovenproof casserole dish. Sprinkle with cracker crumbs. Melt butter in a saucepan. Add sherry and juice and cook 2 minutes. Pour mixture over seafood. Sprinkle with salt, pepper, onion and garlic powder. Lightly sprinkle with paprika and parsley. Bake at 400 degrees 30 minutes.

Yield: 6 servings

Easy Spinach Lasagna

1 (16-ounce) container ricotta cheese
2 cups shredded mozzarella cheese
1 egg
2 (10-ounce) packages frozen chopped spinach, thawed and drained
1 teaspoon salt
⅛ teaspoon pepper
¾ teaspoon dried oregano
1 quart spaghetti sauce
½ (16-ounce) package lasagna noodles, uncooked
¾ cup cold water
Parmesan cheese for topping

Combine ricotta cheese, 1 cup mozzarella cheese, egg, spinach, salt, pepper and oregano. Layer sauce, dry noodles, half ricotta cheese mixture and sauce in a 13 x 9 x 2-inch baking dish. Sprinkle with Parmesan cheese. Continue with a layer of noodles, remainder ricotta cheese mixture, sauce, noodles, sauce, remaining mozzarella cheese and Parmesan cheese. Pour water around the edge of the pan. Cover tightly with foil. Bake at 350 degrees 1 hour, 15 minutes.

Yield: 8 to 10 servings

Cheese Lasagna

RICOTTA FILLING

1 egg
3 cups ricotta cheese

¼ cup finely chopped flat leaf
  parsley
Salt and pepper to taste

Beat egg in a bowl. Stir in ricotta cheese, parsley, salt and pepper. Mix well.

SAUCE

3 tablespoons unsalted butter
1 tablespoon olive oil
1 yellow onion, finely chopped
2 (28-ounce) cans plum tomatoes,
  seeded and chopped with juice
Salt and pepper to taste

6-8 basil leaves, torn into small
  pieces
1 (16-ounce) package lasagna
  noodles, cooked al dente
1 cup grated Parmigiano cheese
½ pound fresh mozzarella cheese,
  thinly sliced

Melt butter with oil in a heavy saucepan. Sauté onions 5 minutes until tender. Add tomatoes and salt. Bring to simmer and cook 45 minutes, stirring occasionally. Stir in basil and pepper. Remove from heat and cool to room temperature. To assemble, spread ¼ cup sauce in the bottom of a 13 x 9 x 2-inch baking dish. Place a layer of noodles over sauce. Spread 1 cup ricotta filling over noodles. Sprinkle with ¼ cup Parmigiano cheese. Scatter one-fourth mozzarella slices on top. Make a second layer of noodles and top with sauce. Layer again with ricotta filling, Parmigiano cheese and mozzarella cheese. Repeat the layers. Make a final layer of noodles, sauce and grated cheese and mozzarella cheese. (May cover and refrigerate at this point before baking.) Bake at 375 degrees 45 minutes until bubbly and top is browned. If lasagna has come straight from the refrigerator, need to bake 1 hour, 15 minutes. Remove from the oven and cool 10 minutes. Reheat any remaining sauce. Cut into squares and serve with sauce and grated cheese.

Yield: 8 servings

Eggplant Lasagna

2 large eggplants, cut into
¼-inch slices
Salt, pepper and garlic powder
to taste
2 cups whole milk ricotta cheese
1 egg
½ teaspoon salt
¼ teaspoon pepper

1 cup red sauce, preferably
homemade
1 large bag spinach, rinsed and
wilted
1 (7 to 10-ounce) jar roasted red
peppers, thinly sliced
6 ounces herbed goat cheese,
crumbled
1 cup shredded mozzarella cheese

Place eggplant slices on greased baking sheets. Sprinkle with salt, pepper and
garlic powder. Bake at 425 degrees 12 minutes. Turn slices over and bake an
additional 12 minutes until lightly browned. Set aside. Combine ricotta cheese,
egg, salt and pepper. Mix well. To assemble, pour ½ cup red sauce on the bottom
of a 13 x 9 x 2-inch baking dish. Top with eggplant. Spread half ricotta mixture
over eggplant. Place half spinach over ricotta. Top with half the red peppers
and half the goat cheese. Repeat layers starting and ending with eggplant layer.
Spread remaining red sauce over eggplant. Cover with foil. Bake at 350 degrees
35 minutes. Remove foil and top with mozzarella cheese. Bake an additional
10 minutes or until cheese melts. Cut into squares and serve.

Yield: 8 to 10 servings

*When serving this dish, it is nice to place a small amount of red sauce on the plate
and place the eggplant square on top. Sprinkle with Parmesan cheese if desired.*

Eggplant Rollatine

2 medium eggplant, peeled and cut lengthwise into ¼-inch strips
Vegetable oil
Salt, pepper and garlic powder to taste
1 cup ricotta cheese
1 large egg

½ teaspoon salt
¼ teaspoon pepper
1 teaspoon minced parsley
¼ cup grated Parmesan cheese plus more for topping
2 cups red sauce
1 cup shredded mozzarella cheese

Place eggplant on an oiled baking sheet. Sprinkle with salt, pepper and garlic powder. Bake at 425 degrees 10 minutes on each side until lightly browned. Combine ricotta cheese, egg, salt, pepper, parsley and Parmesan cheese. Mix well. To assemble, place 1 teaspoon ricotta mixture in the center of each eggplant strip. Gently roll up. Spread a thin layer of red sauce in the bottom of a 13 x 9 x 2-inch baking dish. Place rollatines (eggplant rolls) loose end down. Sprinkle with Parmesan cheese and top with red sauce. Bake at 350 degrees 45 minutes. Top with mozzarella cheese and bake an additional 5 minutes or until cheese melts.

Yield: 14 Rollatines

Moussaka

EGGPLANT

1 large eggplant, peeled and cut into 1-inch chunks	½ teaspoon salt
6 tablespoons vegetable oil	½ teaspoon pepper

On a baking sheet, toss eggplant with oil, salt and pepper. Spread in a single layer. Roast at 450 degrees 20 to 30 minutes until soft and golden browned. Arrange in an even layer in a buttered 4-quart baking dish.

SAUCE

1 tablespoon olive oil	2 teaspoons tomato paste
2 onions, chopped	⅓ cup chopped flat leaf parsley
2 garlic cloves, minced	2 teaspoons dried oregano
1 pound ground beef or lamb	1 teaspoon cinnamon
1 (28-ounce) can whole tomatoes, drained	¼ teaspoon salt
	¼ teaspoon pepper

Heat oil in a saucepan. Add onions, garlic and meat. Cook 5 to 7 minutes until meat is browned. Add tomatoes, tomato paste, parsley, oregano, cinnamon, salt and pepper. Simmer, crushing tomatoes with a spoon, 15 minutes. Spread over eggplant.

RICOTTA CHEESE

1 (9-ounce) container ricotta cheese	⅛ teaspoon salt
4 ounces feta cheese	⅛ teaspoon pepper
1 large egg	

Combine ricotta cheese, feta cheese, egg, salt and pepper. Spread over sauce sealing edges. Broil 5 to 10 minutes until lightly browned. Serve hot.

Yield: 6 servings

Serve the Moussaka with a delicious salad.

Pasta Diablo

1 pound boneless, skinless
    chicken breast halves, cut
    into small strips
3 tablespoons olive oil
1 sweet red pepper, sliced
1 bell pepper, sliced

1 medium onion, sliced
Juice of 1 lime
1 (24-ounce) jar salsa
1 teaspoon Tabasco sauce
Hot cooked linguine

Sauté chicken in oil until browned. Add peppers and onions. Cook until tender. Add juice and some water. Bring to boil. Stir in salsa and Tabasco. Boil 15 minutes. Serve over linguine.

Yield: 4 servings

Hot and delicious! To reduce "heat", use mild salsa and ½ teaspoon Tabasco. Enjoy!

Pasta with Tomato Vodka Sauce

2 tablespoons olive oil
½ cup chopped onions
1 garlic clove, finely chopped
1 (28-ounce) can plum tomatoes
    with juice
½ cup vodka
1 teaspoon crushed red pepper

½ cup heavy cream, at room
    temperature
Salt to taste
2 tablespoons dried parsley
12 ounces fresh or dry pasta,
    cooked al dente

Heat oil in a skillet. Sauté onions 5 minutes. Stir in garlic. Add tomatoes, vodka and red pepper. Break tomatoes with a spoon. Cook 15 minutes until reduced by one-third and thickened. Stir in cream and simmer 5 minutes. Add salt and parsley. Toss sauce and pasta. Serve immediately.

Yield: 4 servings

Pasta Primavera

1 zucchini, thinly sliced
1 yellow squash, cut into thin
   strips
1 sweet red pepper, diced
½ cup peapods
½ cup shredded carrots
1 cup mushrooms, sliced
1 garlic clove, minced

1 cup half-and-half, at room
   temperature
1 teaspoon salt
1 teaspoon dried basil
Pepper to taste
1 (7-ounce) package penne,
   ziti, fusilli or linguine,
   cooked al dente
1½ cups Parmesan cheese

Sauté zucchini, squash, peppers, peapods, carrots, mushrooms and garlic until tender. Remove vegetables with a slotted spoon. Add half-and-half to skillet. Stir in salt, basil and pepper. Stir until boiling. Reduce heat and simmer 2 minutes. Return vegetables to sauce. Add pasta and cheese. Gently toss and serve.

Yield: 4 servings

Instead of 1 sweet red pepper, may use a mixture of red, yellow and orange peppers. The colors make this dish very pleasing to the eye.

Tortellini Primavera

1 tablespoon olive oil
1½ cups sliced mushrooms
1 cup thinly sliced sweet
   red peppers
1 (12-ounce) container
   Alfredo sauce

1 cup frozen peas
⅛ teaspoon cayenne pepper
1 (9-ounce) package tortellini,
   cooked and drained

Heat oil in a saucepan. Sauté mushrooms and peppers 5 minutes until tender. Stir in Alfredo sauce, peas and cayenne. Heat thoroughly. Toss with pasta.

Yield: 4 servings

Penne Gorgonzola

¼ cup olive oil
1 teaspoon dried basil, crumbled
1 teaspoon dried oregano, crumbled
1 teaspoon minced garlic
½ teaspoon crushed red pepper flakes
1 cup firmly packed spinach leaves, rinsed, dried and chopped

¼ cup roasted red pepper, drained and chopped
¼ cup chopped black olives
4 canned artichoke hearts, halved
½ cup dry red wine
½ cup crumbled Gorgonzola cheese
8 ounces penne pasta, cooked al dente

Heat oil, basil, oregano, garlic and red pepper flakes in a skillet. Cook 30 seconds. Add spinach, peppers, olives and artichokes and cook 2 minutes. Stir in wine and boil 2 to 3 minutes until reduced by half. Stir in half Gorgonzola cheese. Spoon sauce over cooked pasta and toss well. Top with remaining Gorgonzola cheese.

Yield: 4 servings

Egg-Olive Sandwiches

12 large hard-cooked eggs, chopped
1 (6-ounce) jar Spanish olives, chopped

⅔-1 cup mayonnaise
Salt and pepper to taste
24 slices white or whole wheat bread

Combine eggs and olives. Stir in mayonnaise ⅓ cup at a time until moistened. Sprinkle with salt and pepper. Trim crust from bread. Spread 12 slices with egg mixture. Top with plain slices. Cut in halves or quarters.

Yield: 48 tea sandwiches

Great to make with leftover Easter eggs.

Hot Brown

2 tablespoons butter
¼ cup flour
2 cups milk
1 cup grated Cheddar cheese
¼ cup grated Parmesan cheese
Pinch of nutmeg
½ teaspoon white pepper
8 slices trimmed bread

1 pound sliced roast turkey breast
  (from leftover roast turkey)
8 slices beefsteak tomatoes, grilled
  in frying pan until just cooked
  through
8 slices cooked bacon
4 ounces grated Parmesan cheese

Melt butter in a saucepan; blend in flour. Add milk, Cheddar cheese, Parmesan cheese, nutmeg and pepper. Stir constantly until smooth and thickened. Set aside.

Arrange bread on a baking sheet lined with nonstick aluminum foil. Place turkey slices on bread and cover with hot cheese sauce. Top with tomato and sprinkle with Parmesan cheese. Place under broiler and cook until bubbly and top is golden brown. Top with sliced bacon.

Yield: 8 servings

Basil and Tomato Frittata

1 (8-ounce) package shredded
  sharp Cheddar cheese
1 tablespoon all-purpose flour
¼ cup shredded Monterey Jack
  cheese
6 eggs, beaten

½ cup half-and-half
1 tablespoon Worcestershire
  sauce
1 large tomato, diced
3 tablespoons chopped basil

Toss Cheddar cheese with flour. Spread in the bottom of a 9-inch pie plate. Sprinkle Jack cheese on top. Whisk together eggs and half-and-half. Stir in Worcestershire sauce. Pour egg mixture over cheese. Top with tomatoes and basil. Bake at 350 degrees 35 to 40 minutes.

Yield: 4 to 5 servings

Cuban Sandwich

2 teaspoons butter
4 (8-inch) club sandwich rolls
Prepared mustard
¾ pound deli baked ham or
    pork slices

16 slices kosher dill pickles or
    8 sandwich slices
½ pound provolone and or
    Swiss cheese slices
Mayonnaise to taste

Heat butter in a nonstick skillet. Split each roll horizontally in half. Lightly spread mustard on bottom. Top each with one-fourth of ham, pickles and cheese. Lightly spread top with mayonnaise and place on top of sandwich. Arrange sandwiches in center of hot skillet. Place a heavy skillet on top of sandwiches. Cook 4 to 5 minutes turning sandwiches once until cheese melts and rolls are browned.

Yield: 4 servings

Our first encounter with a Cuban sandwich was while we were visiting our cousin, Tillie in Florida. She was able to purchase Cuban bread but the soft hero or club rolls depending on where you live will do just fine. Tillie was a special lady that made you feel at home and cooking delicious meals was effortless.

Vegetable Baguettes

PARSLEY DRESSING

2 garlic cloves, chopped
Juice of 2 lemons
Pepper to taste
1 cup finely chopped flat
    leaf parsley

½ cup finely chopped watercress
    leaves
¾ cup extra-virgin olive oil

Combine garlic, juice and pepper. Add parsley and watercress. Whisk in oil. Set aside.

BAGUETTES

2 yellow peppers, halved and
    seeded
2 sweet red peppers, halved
    and seeded
1 cup coarsely chopped flat leaf
    parsley, loosely packed
1 cup coarsely chopped watercress
    leaves

¾ cup pitted and coarsely chopped,
    oil-cured black olives
1 pint cherry tomatoes, quartered
1 bunch green onions, thinly
    sliced
¼ cup drained capers
Salt and pepper to taste
3 crusty baguettes

Broil peppers skin side up until well browned. Transfer to a plastic bag until cool. Save liquid from peppers. Peel skin and discard. Cut into long strips and save liquid. Place peppers and liquid in a bowl. Add parsley, watercress, olives, tomatoes, green onions and capers. Sprinkle with salt and pepper. Add enough parsley dressing to coat and mix well. Slice baguettes in half lengthwise, leaving a hinge on one side. Scoop out middle and discard. Leave a little bread near the edges so filling does not leak out. Brush inside of baguette with dressing. Pack marinated vegetables into baguettes and close up. Wrap tightly in plastic wrap and place on a baking sheet. Refrigerate. Place a second baking sheet on top of baguettes. Weigh down with heavy books 1 to 3 hours. Slice baguettes and serve.

Yield: 12 servings

Eggs Divine

1 pound bulk sausage
1 medium onion, chopped
2 jalapeño peppers, minced
6 eggs
3 tablespoons sour cream

¼ teaspoon salt
¼ teaspoon pepper
1 cup shredded Cheddar cheese
1 cup shredded Monterey Jack
  cheese

Brown sausage with onions and peppers. Drain. Spoon mixture into a greased 11 x 7 x 2-inch baking dish. Combine eggs, sour cream, salt and pepper in a blender. Process 1 minute. Pour over sausage mixture. Top with Cheddar and Monterey Jack cheese. Bake at 325 degrees 30 minutes.

Yield: 8 servings

Hotel Del Coronado Quiche

6 cups shredded Monterey
  Jack cheese
½ medium onion, chopped
¼ cup thinly sliced sweet
  red pepper
4 tablespoons butter
8 ounces smoked turkey,
  julienned

8 eggs, beaten
1¾ cups milk
½ cup all-purpose flour
2 tablespoons snipped chives,
  basil, tarragon or thyme
1 tablespoon snipped parsley

Sprinkle 3 cups cheese in the bottom of a 13 x 9 x 2-inch baking dish. Sauté onions and peppers in butter until tender. Drain well. Spread over cheese. Arrange turkey over vegetables. Top with remaining cheese. Cover and refrigerate overnight. Combine eggs, milk, flour, chives and parsley. Pour over cheese layer. Bake at 350 degrees 45 minutes. Cool 10 minutes before serving.

Yield: 12 servings

Rosita's Spanish Eggs

1 medium onion, chopped
3 tablespoons vegetable oil
1 (14½-ounce) can diced or
    stewed tomatoes, undrained

6 eggs, slightly beaten
1 teaspoon salt
½ teaspoon pepper

Sauté onions in oil until tender. Add tomatoes and liquid. Simmer 10 minutes until liquid is reduced by half. Add eggs, salt and pepper. Scramble eggs into mixture. Cook until eggs are light and fluffy.

Yield: 2 servings

Ratatouille and Goat Cheese Omelet

1 tablespoon vegetable oil
1 red onion, finely chopped
1 teaspoon minced garlic
½ eggplant, peeled and cubed
1 small zucchini, chopped
2 tomatoes, chopped
1 tablespoon minced parsley

½ teaspoon dried tarragon
1 teaspoon dried basil
8 eggs
¼ cup milk
4 tablespoons butter
8 ounces goat cheese, crumbled

Heat oil in large skillet. Sauté onions and garlic until tender. Add eggplant, zucchini, tomatoes, parsley, tarragon and basil. Cook 15 to 20 minutes or until soft. Whisk together eggs and milk in a bowl. Heat 1 tablespoon butter in a separate large skillet. Pour in one-fourth egg mixture. When egg thickens add one-fourth vegetable mixture and one-fourth goat cheese. Fold over cooked egg and place on a warm plate. Cover and keep warm. Repeat with butter, egg batter, vegetable mixture and cheese to make three more omelets.

Yield: 4 servings

Breads & Muffins

*"Bread is like dresses, hats and shoes —
in other words, essential!"*

~ EMILY POST

Catch Me If You Can Muffins

TOPPING

⅓ cup all-purpose flour	3 tablespoons butter
¼ cup packed brown sugar	1 teaspoon cinnamon
¼ cup chopped walnuts	

Combine flour, brown sugar, walnuts, butter and cinnamon until crumbly. Set aside.

MUFFINS

1 cup raisins	2 cups all-purpose flour
½ cup boiling water	1½ teaspoons baking soda
5 tablespoons butter, softened	1 teaspoon cinnamon
¾ cup molasses	1 teaspoon ground ginger
1 egg	½ teaspoon salt

Cover raisins with boiling water. Let stand 5 minutes. In a separate bowl, beat butter and molasses until fluffy. Add egg and beat well. Stir in flour, baking soda, cinnamon, ginger and salt. Blend until dry ingredients are moistened. Gently stir in raisins and water. Spoon batter into greased and floured or paper-lined muffin cups, filling three-fourths full. Sprinkle with topping. Bake at 375 degrees 20 to 25 minutes or until tester comes out clean. Cool 5 minutes and remove from pan. Serve warm.

Yield: 12 muffins

Blackberry Muffins

CRUMB TOPPING

¼ cup all-purpose flour

2 tablespoons packed brown sugar

Dash of cinnamon

2 tablespoons butter, softened

Combine flour, brown sugar, cinnamon and butter until crumbly. Set aside.

MUFFINS

½ cup vanilla yogurt

¼ cup milk

⅓ cup packed dark brown sugar

¼ cup vegetable oil

1 egg

1¾ cups all-purpose flour

1 tablespoon baking powder

¼ teaspoon salt

¼ teaspoon baking soda

1 cup blackberries

Blend yogurt, milk, brown sugar, oil and egg. In a separate bowl, combine flour, baking powder, salt and baking soda. Add dry ingredients to creamed mixture. Mix well. Fold in berries. Spoon batter into well greased muffin cups. Top with crumb topping. Bake at 400 degrees 20 to 25 minutes. Remove from pan to cool.

Yield: 10 to 12 muffins

Cranberry Upside-Down Muffins

¾ cup whole berry cranberry sauce
¼ cup packed brown sugar
2 cups all-purpose flour
2 tablespoons sugar
3 teaspoons baking powder

½ teaspoon salt
1 cup milk
¼ cup vegetable oil
1 teaspoon orange zest
2 egg whites

Spoon 1 tablespoon cranberry sauce into each muffin cup. Top with 1 teaspoon brown sugar. Combine flour, sugar, baking powder and salt in a large bowl. In a separate bowl, blend milk, oil, zest and egg whites. Add to flour mixture all at once. Stir until dry ingredients are moistened. Divide batter evenly among muffin cups. Bake at 400 degrees 14 to 18 minutes or until tester comes out clean. Cool in pan 1 minute. Rim the edges of pan to loosen muffin. Invert muffins onto a wire rack with wax paper underneath. Cool 5 minutes. Serve warm.

Yield: 12 muffins

Other variations are possible. Consider using peach, apricot or another favorite preserves to replace cranberry sauce.

Ginger Rhubarb Muffins

2¼ cups all-purpose flour
2 teaspoons baking powder
1 teaspoon baking soda
½ teaspoon salt
2 tablespoons finely chopped
   crystallized ginger

¾ cup sugar
½ cup milk
½ cup sour cream
⅓ cup vegetable oil
1 egg
1 cup finely chopped rhubarb

Combine flour, baking powder, baking soda, salt and ginger. In a separate bowl, blend sugar, milk, sour cream, oil and egg. Stir in rhubarb. Add to dry ingredients and stir until moistened. Spoon batter into muffin cups, filling three-fourths full. Bake at 400 degrees 15 minutes or until tester comes out clean. Cool in pan 5 minutes. Remove to cool completely.

Yield: 16 muffins

Lemon-Dipped Blueberry Muffins

1¾ cups all-purpose flour
½ cup sugar
2½ teaspoons baking powder
¾ teaspoon salt
1 egg, well beaten
⅓ cup vegetable oil
¾ cup milk

1 cup blueberries, rinsed
  and dried
2 tablespoons sugar
2 teaspoons lemon zest
2 tablespoons butter, melted
¼ teaspoon lemon juice
Sugar for topping

Combine flour, sugar, baking powder and salt. Make a well in the center. Blend egg, oil and milk. Add to well and stir until moistened. Toss blueberries with sugar and zest. Fold berries into batter. Spoon batter into greased and floured muffin cups, filling two-thirds full. Bake at 400 degrees 20 minutes or until golden browned. While baking, blend butter and juice. Dip warm muffins in butter mixture and then in sugar.

Yield: 14 muffins

Lemon Raspberry Streusel Muffins

TOPPING

⅓ cup sugar

2 tablespoons butter, softened

¼ cup all-purpose flour

Combine sugar, flour and butter until crumbly. Set aside.

MUFFINS

2 cups all-purpose flour

½ cup sugar

2 teaspoons baking powder

½ teaspoon baking soda

½ teaspoon salt

1 (8-ounce) container lemon yogurt

½ cup vegetable oil

1 teaspoon lemon zest

2 eggs

1 cup fresh or frozen raspberries, thawed

Combine flour, sugar, baking powder, baking soda and salt. In a separate bowl, blend yogurt, oil, zest and eggs. Add to dry ingredients. Stir until moistened. Fold in berries. Spoon batter into muffin cups, filling three-fourths full. Sprinkle with topping. Bake at 400 degrees 20 minutes. Cool 5 minutes in pan. Remove to cool completely.

Yield: 12 muffins or 20 mini muffins

Peach-Pocket Cornmeal Muffins

1 cup all-purpose flour
1 cup cornmeal
1 tablespoon sugar
1 tablespoon baking powder
¼ teaspoon salt
⅔ cup milk

4 tablespoons unsalted butter, melted and cooled
1 large egg, room temperature
⅓ cup maple syrup
½ cup peach preserves

Sift together flour, cornmeal, sugar, baking powder and salt. Make a well in the center. Blend milk, butter, egg and syrup. Pour into well and stir until moistened. Do not over mix. Spoon 1 tablespoon batter into eight greased muffin cups. Make a pocket in the batter with the back of the spoon. Spoon 2 teaspoons preserves into each pocket. Cover with remaining batter to ½-inch from top. Bake at 400 degrees 18 to 20 minutes or until golden browned. Transfer to wire rack to cool slightly. Serve warm.

Yield: 8 muffins

Pear Muffins

2 cups all-purpose flour
¾ cup sugar
2 teaspoons baking soda
½ teaspoon salt
¼ teaspoon cardamom or
  1 teaspoon cinnamon
2 eggs, beaten

½ cup vegetable oil
2 tablespoons milk
1 teaspoon grated ginger
2 medium pears, peeled and finely chopped
¾ cup chopped walnuts
½ cup raisins

Combine flour, sugar, baking soda, salt and cardamom. Make a well in the center. Blend together eggs, oil, milk and ginger. Add to well and stir until moistened. Batter will be thick. Fold in pears, walnuts and raisins. Spoon batter into greased muffin cups, filling three-fourths full. Bake at 350 degrees 20 to 25 minutes or until tester comes out clean. Remove from pan and serve warm.

Yield: 18 muffins

Pumpkin Maple Corn Muffins

1 cup yellow cornmeal	½ cup packed brown sugar
1 cup all-purpose flour	½ cup canned pumpkin
½ teaspoon salt	2 eggs, slightly beaten
2 teaspoons baking powder	½ cup milk or half-and-half
1 teaspoon baking soda	½ cup maple syrup
6 tablespoons butter, softened	

Combine cornmeal, flour, salt, baking powder and baking soda. Make a well in the center and set aside. Cream together butter and brown sugar. Stir in pumpkin and eggs. Add milk and syrup and mix well. Pour pumpkin mixture into well and stir until moistened. Spoon batter into greased muffin cups, filling three-fourths full. Bake at 350 degrees 25 minutes.

Yield: 18 muffins

Great with chili or a cup of tea! Nancy serves it with maple butter from our local dairy! Delicious!

Summer Muffins

3 cups unbleached flour	2 large eggs
1½ cups sugar	2 sticks unsalted butter, melted
1 tablespoon baking powder	1 cup blueberries
½ teaspoon baking soda	½ cup diced strawberries
½ teaspoon salt	½ cup raspberries
3-4 teaspoons cinnamon	½ cup sugar
1¼ cups milk	

Combine flour, sugar, baking powder, baking soda, salt and cinnamon. Make a well in the center. Blend milk and eggs. Pour into well along with butter. Stir quickly to combine. Fold in all berries. Spoon batter into greased or paper-lined muffin cups, filling almost to the top. Sprinkle with sugar. Bake at 375 degrees 20 minutes or until browned.

Yield: 20 muffins

Sweet Potato Muffins

4 tablespoons butter, softened	½ teaspoon salt
½ cup sugar	½ teaspoon cinnamon
1 egg	¼ teaspoon ground nutmeg
⅔ cup canned sweet potatoes, drained and mashed	½ cup milk
	¼ cup chopped nuts, pecans or walnuts
¾ cup all-purpose flour	
2 teaspoons baking powder	1 tablespoon cinnamon-sugar mix

Cream butter and sugar until smooth. Beat in egg and sweet potatoes. Sift together flour, baking powder, salt, cinnamon and nutmeg. Add dry ingredients to creamed mixture alternately with milk. Do not over mix. Stir in nuts. Spoon batter into greased muffin cups, filling to the top. Sprinkle with cinnamon-sugar mixture. Bake at 400 degrees 25 minutes.

Yield: 12 muffins

Key Lime Muffins

2 cups all-purpose flour	¼ cup vegetable oil
1 tablespoon baking powder	⅓ cup milk
½ teaspoon salt	¼ cup Key lime juice
1 cup sugar	1 cup powdered sugar
1 teaspoon lime zest	2-3 tablespoons Key lime juice
2 eggs	

Combine flour, baking powder, salt, sugar and zest. Stir in eggs, oil, milk and juice until moistened. Spoon batter into greased and floured muffin cups, filling three-fourths full. Bake at 400 degrees 15 to 18 minutes or until lightly browned. While baking, blend powdered sugar and juice. Add more juice, 1 teaspoon at a time to reach desired consistency. Drizzle glaze over warm muffins.

Yield: 12 muffins

French Breakfast Muffins

CINNAMON SUGAR TOPPING

1 teaspoon cinnamon

½ cup sugar

½ teaspoon vanilla

Combine cinnamon, sugar and vanilla. Set aside.

MUFFINS

1 large egg, beaten

½ cup milk

5 tablespoons butter, melted

1½ cups plus 2 tablespoons
all-purpose flour

¾ cup sugar

2 teaspoons baking powder

¼ teaspoon salt

¼ teaspoon ground nutmeg

5 tablespoons butter, melted

Blend egg, milk and butter. Combine flour, sugar, baking powder, salt and nutmeg. Add to creamed mixture. Spoon batter into greased muffin cups, filling one-half full. Bake at 400 degrees 15 minutes or until browned. Immediately remove muffins from pan and dip in butter. Roll in cinnamon topping.

Yield: 10 to 12 muffins

Coffee Cake Muffins

TOPPING

3 tablespoons all-purpose flour	2 tablespoons butter
3 tablespoons packed brown sugar	3 tablespoons chopped pecans
¼ teaspoon cinnamon	or walnuts

Combine flour, brown sugar and cinnamon. Cut in butter until crumbly. Stir in nuts.

MUFFINS

1½ cups all-purpose flour	¼ teaspoon baking soda
½ cup sugar	¼ teaspoon salt
1¼ teaspoons baking powder	4 tablespoons butter
½ teaspoon cinnamon	1 egg, beaten
¼ teaspoon ground ginger	½ cup buttermilk

Combine flour, sugar, baking powder, cinnamon, ginger, baking soda and salt. Cut in butter until crumbly. Blend together egg and milk. Add to dry ingredients and stir until moistened. Batter will be lumpy. Spoon batter into greased and floured muffin cups, filling one-third full. Top each with half of the topping. Spoon on remaining batter and then remaining topping. Bake at 400 degrees 15 to 18 minutes or until golden browned. Cool in pan 5 minutes. Remove from pan and serve warm.

Yield: 12 muffins

Maple Walnut Muffins

MUFFINS

1 egg, beaten	3 teaspoons baking powder
½ cup milk	½ teaspoon salt
½ cup maple syrup	¼ cup vegetable oil
½ cup sugar	½ cup chopped walnuts
2 cups all-purpose flour	

Blend egg, milk, syrup and sugar. Stir in flour, baking powder, salt and oil until moistened. Fold in walnuts. Do not over mix. Spoon batter into greased and floured muffin cups, filling two-thirds full. Bake at 400 degrees 15 to 18 minutes.

MAPLE GLAZE

5 tablespoons maple syrup	1 cup powdered sugar

In a measuring cup, mix syrup and powdered sugar until smooth. Drizzle over muffins.

Yield: 12 muffins

Blueberry-Banana Bread

1 cup sugar	2½ teaspoons baking powder
2 tablespoons butter, softened	½ teaspoon baking soda
1 egg	1 teaspoon salt
3 ripe bananas, mashed	½ cup chopped walnuts
½ cup orange juice	½ cup blueberries
2 cups all-purpose flour	

Cream sugar and butter. Beat in egg. Add bananas, beating well. Stir in juice. Sift together flour, baking powder, baking soda and salt. Stir dry ingredients into banana mixture. Add walnuts and blueberries. Pour batter into a greased 9 x 5-inch loaf pan. Let stand 15 minutes. Bake at 350 degrees 1 hour.

Yield: 1 loaf

Star Spangled Muffins

1 stick butter, softened
1 cup sugar
2 cups blueberries
1 cup all-purpose flour
½ cup dried cranberries

1 cup milk
2 eggs
2 cups all-purpose flour
2 tablespoons baking powder
Sugar for topping

Cream butter and sugar until smooth. Set aside. Place blueberries in a deep bowl. Add flour and gently toss to coat. Stir in cranberries. In a separate bowl, beat together milk, eggs, flour and baking powder. Add to creamed mixture and beat well. Fold in berries. Spoon batter into paper lined muffin cups, filling two-thirds full. Sprinkle with sugar. Bake at 350 degrees 23 to 25 minutes.

Yield: 24 muffins

A Fourth of July tradition!

Armenian Apricot Nut Loaf

3 eggs
1 teaspoon vanilla
¾ cup all-purpose flour
½ teaspoon baking soda
¼ teaspoon baking powder

Dash of salt
¾ cup packed dark brown sugar
2 cups dried apricots
2 cups prunes
2 cups whole walnuts

Beat eggs and vanilla. Set aside. Combine flour, baking soda, baking powder, salt and brown sugar. Stir in apricots, prunes and walnuts. Add egg mixture and mix well. Spray a 9 x 5-inch loaf pan with cooking spray. Line with wax paper, covering all sides. Trim excess paper over top. Press batter into pan. Bake at 325 degrees 55 to 60 minutes. Cool completely. Invert and peel away wax paper and serve.

Yield: 1 loaf

We were given this recipe by our dear friend Rose.

Mommy's Banana Bread

1 stick butter, softened
1 cup sugar
2 eggs
3 bananas, mashed

2 cups all-purpose flour
1 teaspoon baking soda
½ teaspoon salt

Cream butter and sugar until fluffy. Add eggs and beat 1 to 2 minutes. Stir in bananas. Sift together flour, baking soda and salt. Add to banana mixture. Stir with a wooden spoon 30 seconds. Pour batter into a greased and floured 9 x 5-inch loaf pan. Bake at 375 degrees 15 minutes. Reduce to 350 degrees and bake an additional 45 minutes.

Yield: 1 loaf

There are a lot of banana bread recipes out there. This is by far the best we have ever tasted and of course it is our Mother's recipe which makes it even more special.

Mom's Dark Date Nut Bread

1 (10-ounce) package dates,
  chopped
1½ cups boiling water
2 tablespoons Crisco shortening
1 cup sugar
¼ cup packed dark brown sugar

1 teaspoon salt
1 egg, well beaten
2¾ cups all-purpose flour
1 teaspoon baking soda
1 cup chopped walnuts
2 teaspoons vanilla

Combine dates, water, shortening, sugar, brown sugar and salt. Mix well and set aside. When cooled, stir in egg, flour, baking soda, nuts and vanilla. Pour batter into a 9 x 5-inch loaf pan. Bake at 350 degrees 1 hour, 15 minutes.

Yield: 1 loaf

This is the best date nut bread ever. It is especially good when served with cream cheese.

Blueberry Lemon Bread

BREAD

1½ cups all-purpose flour
1 teaspoon baking powder
¼ teaspoon salt
6 tablespoons butter, softened
1½ cups sugar

2 eggs
2 tablespoons lemon zest
½ cup milk
1½ cups blueberries

Combine flour, baking powder and salt. In a separate bowl, cream butter and sugar until fluffy. Add eggs, beating well. Stir in zest. Add dry ingredients alternately with milk to creamed mixture. Fold in berries. Pour batter into a 9 x 5-inch loaf pan. Bake at 325 degrees 1 hour, 15 minutes or until golden browned.

GLAZE

⅓ cup sugar

3 tablespoons lemon juice

Combine sugar and juice in a saucepan. Bring to boil. Pierce holes in bread. Pour glaze over bread allowing glaze to soak in. Cool 30 minutes.

Yield: 1 loaf

Irish Soda Bread

2 cups all-purpose flour
1 cup sugar
1 teaspoon cream of tartar
½ teaspoon baking soda
Dash of salt

2 eggs, beaten
1 (8-ounce) container sour cream
1 stick butter, melted
1 cup raisins

Sift together flour, sugar, cream of tartar, baking soda and salt. Add eggs, sour cream and butter. Mix well. Stir in raisins. Pour batter into an 8-inch round pan. Bake at 350 degrees 55 minutes.

Yield: 8 to 10 servings

Dried Cherry Tea Bread

¾ cup sugar
1 stick butter, softened
1 teaspoon vanilla
1 cup buttermilk
2 eggs
1 cup dried cherries, chopped

1 teaspoon lemon zest
2 cups all-purpose flour
½ teaspoon baking powder
½ teaspoon baking soda
½ teaspoon salt
½ teaspoon cardamom

Beat sugar and butter until light and fluffy. Beat in vanilla. Add buttermilk and eggs and beat well. Combine cherries, zest, flour, baking powder, baking soda, salt and cardamom. Add to creamed mixture just until moistened. Pour batter into a greased and floured 9 x 5-inch or 8 x 4-inch loaf pan. Bake at 350 degrees 48 to 50 minutes (8 x 4-inch pan, 55 minutes to 1 hour, 15 minutes). Rim edges of pan with a knife. Cool in pan on a wire rack 15 minutes. Remove bread to rack to cool completely. Wrap tightly and store in refrigerator.

Yield: 1 loaf

Lemon Tea Bread

1½ cups all-purpose flour
1 cup sugar
1 teaspoon baking powder
½ teaspoon salt

1 stick butter, melted
½ cup milk
2 eggs
Zest of 1 lemon

Combine flour, sugar, baking powder and salt. Blend butter, milk, eggs and zest until smooth. Add to dry ingredients and stir until moistened. Pour batter into a greased 8 x 4-inch loaf pan. Bake at 350 degrees 45 minutes or until tester comes out clean. Cool in pan 10 minutes. Remove from pan and cool completely.

Yield: 10 to 12 servings

If you are looking for a basic and easy lemon bread, this one is for you!

Spicy Cape Cod Pumpkin Bread

1½ cups sugar	¼ teaspoon ground allspice
1 teaspoon baking soda	1 cup pumpkin
1⅔ cups all-purpose flour	½ cup vegetable oil
¼ teaspoon baking powder	½ cup water
½ teaspoon cinnamon	2 eggs, well beaten
¼ teaspoon ground nutmeg	½ cup raisins
¼ teaspoon ground ginger	½ cup chopped walnuts
¼ teaspoon ground cloves	

Combine sugar, baking soda, flour, baking powder, cinnamon, nutmeg, ginger, cloves and allspice. Mix well. Add pumpkin, oil, water, eggs, raisins and walnuts. Mix until well blended. Pour batter into a greased and floured 9 x 5-inch loaf pan. Bake at 350 degrees 1 hour.

Yield: 1 loaf

Strawberry Moon Bread

1 stick butter, softened	½ teaspoon baking soda
1½ cups sugar	½ cup sour cream
1 teaspoon vanilla	3 cups all-purpose flour
1 teaspoon salt	½ cup chopped nuts
1 teaspoon lemon juice	1 cup strawberry preserves
4 eggs	1 tablespoon red food coloring

Cream butter, sugar, vanilla, salt and juice. Beat in eggs, one at a time. Blend baking soda and sour cream. Add to creamed mixture. Fold in flour, nuts, preserves and food coloring. Mix well. Pour batter into two greased 9 x 5-inch loaf pans. Bake at 350 degrees 35 to 40 minutes or until bread separates from pan.

Yield: 2 loaves

The "strawberry moon" occurs in the month of June during the strawberry season. Hence the name of this bread.

Yankee Garlic Bread

1 loaf Italian or French bread	1 shallot, finely chopped
3 tablespoons unsalted butter, room temperature	3 tablespoons Parmesan cheese
1 teaspoon olive oil	1 teaspoon pepper
3-4 garlic cloves, finely chopped	¼ cup finely chopped parsley

Cut bread diagonally into ¾- to 1-inch thick slices. Place on a baking sheet. Blend butter, oil, garlic, shallot, cheese and pepper. Mix well with a fork. Lightly spread butter mixture over bread. Bake at 425 degrees 6 to 9 minutes or until golden browned. Remove from oven and sprinkle with parsley. Serve warm.

Yield: 8 servings

A favorite of Mickey Mantle's.

Diamond, Ruby, Emerald and Sapphire Scones

1½ cups all-purpose flour	½ cup buttermilk
¾ cup whole wheat flour	½ cup dried cranberries
¼ cup sugar	½ cup dried blueberries
1 tablespoon baking powder	½ cup chopped pistachios
¼ teaspoon salt	1 teaspoon finely grated orange zest
1 stick unsalted butter, chilled	2 tablespoons white sugar crystals
1 large egg, room temperature	

Whisk together both flours, sugar, baking powder and salt. Cut in butter with a pastry blender until crumbly. Make a well in the center. Blend egg and buttermilk. Pour into well and stir until moistened. Fold in berries, pistachios and zest. Do not over mix. Spoon batter into six greased and floured heart-shaped muffin cups. Sprinkle with sugar. Bake at 375 degrees 15 to 20 minutes. Transfer scones to a wire rack and cool slightly. Serve warm.

Yield: 6 scones

Middlebury Scones

1½ cups all-purpose flour	¾ cup raisins or dried cranberries
1½ cups cake flour	4 eggs
⅓ cup sugar	1 cup milk
1½ teaspoons salt	½ cup buttermilk
3 tablespoons baking powder	1 egg, for egg wash
2 sticks butter, cubed and chilled	Melted butter and powdered sugar

Combine flour, cake flour, sugar, salt and baking powder. Cut in butter with pastry blender. In a separate bowl, combine raisins, eggs, milk and buttermilk. Add to dry ingredients and mix well. Shape into a ball. Roll out dough on a floured surface to ½-inch thick. Cut dough with a biscuit cutter. Brush tops with egg wash. Place on a greased or paper lined baking sheet. Bake at 425 degrees 15 to 20 minutes or until golden browned. Remove from oven, brush with melted butter and dust with powdered sugar.

Yield: 2 dozen scones

*"There are few hours in life more agreeable than
the hour dedicated to the ceremony known as afternoon tea."*

~ HENRY JAMES

Maple Scones

3 cups all-purpose flour	2 eggs, beaten
1½ tablespoons baking powder	½ cup dark maple syrup
¾ teaspoon salt	⅓ cup heavy cream
1 stick butter	1 cup chopped walnuts

Combine flour, baking powder and salt. Cut in butter with a pastry blender. Make a well in the center. In a separate bowl, whisk together eggs, syrup and cream. Add to well and mix until moistened. Stir in walnuts. Gather the dough into a ball. Roll dough out between two pieces of wax paper into a circle to 1½-inch thick. Cut into 8 pie-shaped pieces and place on a greased and floured baking sheet. Brush the tops with syrup. Bake at 375 degrees 20 minutes.

Yield: 8 scones

Heart-Shape Cornmeal Biscuits

1¼ cups all-purpose flour	5 tablespoons butter
¾ cup cornmeal	1 teaspoon lemon zest
¼ cup sugar	⅔ cup buttermilk or sour milk
2 teaspoons baking powder	1 teaspoon vanilla
¼ teaspoon baking soda	1 teaspoon sugar
¼ teaspoon salt	1 teaspoon cornmeal

Combine flour, cornmeal, sugar, baking powder, baking soda and salt. Cut in butter with a pastry blender until crumbly. Add zest. Make a well in the center. Whisk together buttermilk and vanilla. Add dry ingredients and stir until moistened. Turn dough out onto a floured surface. Quickly knead 10 to 12 times until dough is smooth. Roll to ½-inch thickness. Cut dough with a floured 2-inch heart shape cutter. Dip cutter into flour between cuts. Arrange biscuits so they are just touching on an ungreased or paper lined baking sheet. Sprinkle with sugar and cornmeal. Bake at 400 degrees 10 to 12 minutes or until golden browned. Remove and serve warm.

Yield: 12 to 15 biscuits

Breakfast At Tiffany's French Toast

BREAD

1 large loaf French bread, sliced
    1-inch thick
8 eggs
2 cups half-and-half
1 cup milk

1 teaspoon vanilla
2 tablespoons sugar
¼ teaspoon cinnamon
¼ teaspoon ground nutmeg
Dash of salt

Arrange bread in two overlapping rows in a greased 13 x 9 x 2-inch baking dish. Whisk together eggs, half-and-half, milk, vanilla, sugar, cinnamon, nutmeg and salt. Pour mixture over bread. Cover and refrigerate overnight.

PRALINE TOPPING

2 sticks butter
1 cup packed brown sugar
2 tablespoons light corn syrup
½ teaspoon cinnamon

½ teaspoon ground nutmeg
1 cup chopped pecans
Maple syrup for serving

Prior to serving, melt butter in a saucepan. Stir in brown sugar, corn syrup, cinnamon, nutmeg and pecans. Stir constantly until smooth. Spread topping evenly over bread. Bake at 350 degrees 40 minutes or until puffed and golden browned. Serve with warm maple syrup.

Yield: 8 to 10 servings

"I'm just crazy about Tiffany's!"

~ AUDREY HEPBURN

Macadamia French Toast

6 eggs
½ cup milk
¼ teaspoon ground nutmeg
1 cup orange juice
⅓ cup sugar
1 teaspoon vanilla

1 loaf French bread, cut in
  sixteen 1-inch slices
5 tablespoons butter
½ cup chopped macadamia nuts
1 (15-ounce) can cream of coconut

Whisk together eggs, milk, nutmeg, juice, sugar and vanilla. Place bread in two 13 x 9 x 2-inch cake pans. Divide egg mixture between both pans. Cover tightly and refrigerate overnight. All egg mixture will absorb. Spread butter between two baking sheets. Place soaked bread on baking sheets, without sides touching. Sprinkle with nuts. Bake at 400 degrees 20 to 25 minutes or until golden browned. Serve with cream of coconut.

Yield: 8 servings

Gingerbread Pancakes

1 cup all-purpose flour
1 tablespoon baking powder
1 cup packed dark brown sugar
1½ teaspoons baking soda
1 teaspoon salt
1 teaspoon cinnamon
1 teaspoon ground ginger
¼ teaspoon ground nutmeg

⅛ teaspoon ground cloves
½ cup water
½ cup brewed coffee, cold or
  room temperature
4 large eggs
1 stick unsalted butter, melted and
  cooled
¼ cup lemon juice

Combine flour, baking powder, brown sugar, baking soda, salt, cinnamon, ginger, nutmeg and cloves. Stir in water, coffee, eggs, butter and juice. Mix well. Brush griddle with vegetable oil. Pour batter on hot griddle.

Yield: 18 pancakes

Orange Banana Waffles

1 egg white, room temperature	1 egg yolk
1 cup all-purpose flour	½ cup orange juice
1 teaspoon baking powder	⅓ cup mashed banana
⅛ teaspoon salt	4 tablespoons butter, melted and cooled
1 tablespoon sugar	

Beat egg white until stiff and set aside. Combine flour, baking powder, salt and sugar. Blend egg yolk, juice, banana and butter. Add to dry ingredients until moistened. Fold in egg white until blended. Do not over mix. Cook batter on a greased griddle.

Yield: 12 waffles

A great combination once enjoyed by our Daddy.

Lil's Monkey Bread Bites

¼ cup sugar	¼ cup packed light brown sugar
1 tablespoon cinnamon	¼ cup sugar
1 (12-ounce) can refrigerated buttermilk biscuits	1 teaspoon vanilla
1 (6-ounce) can refrigerated buttermilk biscuits	½ cup chopped pecans, toasted
1 stick plus 2 tablespoons butter	Extra large foil muffin cups

Combine sugar and cinnamon in a large bowl. Cut biscuits into quarters. Add to sugar mixture. Toss to coat. Set aside. Melt butter in a saucepan. Add brown sugar and sugar, stirring until sugar dissolves. Remove from heat. Stir in vanilla and pecans. Arrange 5 coated biscuit pieces in lightly greased foil cups. Place in a muffin pan. Drizzle each cup with pecan mixture. Bake at 400 degrees 18 minutes or until golden browned.

Yield: 10 to 12 servings

Decadent Chocolate Nut Waffles

6 tablespoons butter, melted	2 teaspoons baking powder
2 (1-ounce) unsweetened chocolate baking squares	½ teaspoon salt
⅔ cup sugar	¾ cup milk
2 eggs yolks	¼ cup finely chopped walnuts
1 cup all-purpose flour	2 egg whites

Combine butter and chocolate in a bowl. Let cool slightly. Stir in sugar and egg yolks. Mix well. Combine flour, baking powder and salt. Add dry ingredients alternately with milk to chocolate mixture. Add nuts. Beat egg whites until stiff. Fold egg whites into chocolate mixture. Batter will be thick. Add ½ cup batter to heated waffle iron and spread with a spatula. Close waffle iron and bake until ready.

Yield: 20 waffles

Chocolate may cause sticking, so cooking surfaces should be lightly re-oiled before making this recipe. Oil cooking surfaces before preheating waffle iron. A heart-shaped waffle iron is a must as this recipe would make a wonderful Valentine's Day breakfast or topped with ice cream, strawberries and whipped cream for a great dessert.

Pumpkin Harvest Pancakes

2 cups biscuit baking mix	1½ cups undiluted evaporated milk
2 tablespoons packed light brown sugar	½ cup canned pumpkin
2 teaspoons cinnamon	2 tablespoons vegetable oil
1 teaspoon ground allspice	2 eggs
	1 teaspoon vanilla

Combine baking mix, brown sugar, cinnamon and allspice. Stir in milk, pumpkin, oil, eggs and vanilla. Beat until smooth. Pour ¼ to ½ cup batter onto lightly greased griddle. Cook until top surface is bubbly and edges are dry. Turn, cook until golden. Serve hot with maple syrup or honey.

Yield: 16 pancakes

Presidential Waffles

1 stick butter, softened
1 tablespoon sugar
2 egg yolks
1 cup buttermilk

1 cup plus 1 tablespoon sifted
  cake flour
Pinch of salt
2 egg whites, stiffly beaten
4 teaspoons baking powder

Cream butter and sugar. Add egg yolks and beat well. Add milk alternately with flour and salt. When ready to bake, fold in egg whites and baking powder. Batter should be light and fluffy. Bake on a preheated waffle iron. Serve with hot maple syrup and melted butter.

Yield: 12 to 15 waffles

Here is a waffle recipe preferred by President John F. Kennedy.

Orange Pound Cake

1 stick butter, softened
1¼ cups sugar
2 eggs
2 cups all-purpose flour

1½ teaspoons baking powder
1 teaspoon salt
½ cup orange juice

Cream butter and sugar. Add eggs and mix well. Combine flour, baking powder and salt. Add juice alternately with dry ingredients to creamed mixture. Pour batter into a greased and floured 9 x 5-inch loaf pan. Bake at 350 degrees 50 to 60 minutes.

Yield: 1 loaf

This was a favorite of our Uncle Pepe's and is still a family favorite.

Notes

Desserts

"Desserts is stressed spelled backwards."
~ ANONYMOUS

Black Tie Cheesecake

1¼ cups graham cracker crumbs
5⅓ tablespoons butter, melted
¼ cup packed light brown sugar
1 teaspoon cinnamon
4 (8-ounce) packages cream cheese,
  softened
1¼ cups sugar
2 tablespoons all-purpose flour
4 extra large eggs
2 egg yolks
⅓ cup whipping cream

1 teaspoon vanilla
1½ cups coarsely chopped Oreo
  cookies
2 cups sour cream
¼ cup sugar
1 teaspoon vanilla
1 cup whipping cream
1 (8-ounce) package semi-sweet
  chocolate squares, chopped
1 teaspoon vanilla

Combine cracker crumbs, butter, brown sugar and cinnamon. Press into the bottom and up the sides of a 10-inch springform pan. Refrigerate 30 minutes. Beat cream cheese until smooth. Beat in sugar and flour. Add eggs and egg yolks and beat until smooth. Stir in cream and vanilla. Pour half the batter over crust. Top with chopped cookies and remaining batter. Smooth top with spatula. Bake at 425 degrees 15 minutes. Reduce heat to 225 degrees and bake 55 to 60 minutes. Cover loosely with foil if cake begins to brown. Blend sour cream, sugar and vanilla. Pour over cheesecake. Bake at 350 degrees 7 minutes. Cover and refrigerate overnight. Scald cream over high heat. Add chocolate and vanilla. Cook 1 minute, stirring constantly. Remove from heat and stir until chocolate melts. Refrigerate 10 minutes. Place cheesecake on a serving platter. Remove from springform pan. Pour chocolate mixture over top allowing glaze to drip down sides. Garnish with Oreo halves on the sides and a cherry on the center. Refrigerate until ready to serve.

Yield: 20 servings

Santa Baby Chocolate Cake

CAKE

1 stick butter, softened
1 cup sugar
4 eggs

1 (16-ounce) can chocolate syrup
1 tablespoon almond extract
1 cup all-purpose flour

Line the bottom of a 9-inch round pan with wax paper. Grease the sides. Beat butter and sugar until smooth. Beat in eggs. Add syrup, extract and flour. Beat until blended. Pour batter into prepared pan. Bake at 350 degrees 40 to 45 minutes. Cool in pan for 10 minutes. Invert cake onto wire rack. Remove wax paper. Place a piece of wax paper under rack to catch chocolate drippings.

GLAZE

⅓ cup seedless raspberry jam

Spoon jam into a saucepan. Bring to boil. Reduce heat and simmer 2 minutes. Cool. Spread jam over top of cake.

FROSTING

¼ cup heavy cream
½ cup semi-sweet chocolate chips
½ teaspoon instant coffee powder

¼ cup sliced almonds, toasted
Sweet whipped cream

Combine cream, chips and coffee powder in a saucepan. Cook and stir over low heat until chocolate melts. Spread over top and sides of cake. With two large spatulas, lift cake to a platter. Gently press almonds into the sides. Cut small slices and top with whipped cream.

Yield: 8 to 10 servings

Santa Baby will hurry down the chimney for this decadent chocolate cake. A compliment to this dessert would be a vintage Port Wine.

Simple Devil's Food Cake

1½ cups all-purpose flour	2 large eggs
1¼ cups sugar	1 cup low-fat buttermilk
1¼ teaspoons baking soda	1 teaspoon vanilla
1 teaspoon salt	1⅓ sticks butter, melted
½ cup unsweetened cocoa powder	Powdered sugar

Butter a 13 x 9 x 2-inch baking dish. Line the bottom with wax or parchment paper. Butter paper. Whisk together flour, sugar, baking soda, salt and cocoa. Add eggs, buttermilk, vanilla and butter. Beat on low speed until moistened. Beat on medium speed 3 minutes until smooth. Pour into prepared pan. Bake at 350 degrees 25 minutes or until tester comes out clean. Cool in pan 10 minutes. Invert onto a wire rack. Remove paper and reinvert to cool completely. Dust with powdered sugar.

Yield: 12 servings

Hot Fudge Sundae Cake

1 cup all-purpose flour	1 teaspoon vanilla
¾ cup sugar	1 cup chopped pecans
2 tablespoons cocoa powder	1 cup packed brown sugar
2 tablespoons baking powder	¼ cup cocoa powder
¼ teaspoon salt	1¾ cups very hot water
½ cup milk	Favorite ice cream
2 tablespoons vegetable oil	

Combine flour, sugar, cocoa, baking powder and salt. Stir in milk, oil and vanilla until smooth. Add nuts. Spread batter into a 9 x 9 x 2-inch baking dish. Sprinkle with brown sugar and cocoa. Pour hot water over batter. Bake at 350 degrees 40 minutes. While warm, spoon cake into dishes. Top with ice cream. Spoon sauce from pan over ice cream.

Yield: 8 servings

Hotel Del Milky Way Layer Cake

CAKE

8 (1¾-ounce) Milky Way candy bars
1 stick butter
2 cups sugar
2 sticks butter, softened
4 eggs, well beaten
2½ cups all-purpose flour
½ teaspoon baking soda
1¼ cups buttermilk
1 teaspoon vanilla
1 cup chopped pecans
Powdered sugar

Melt candy bars with butter. Remove from heat and cool. Cream sugar and butter. Add eggs and cooled candy mixture. Sift together flour and baking soda. Add flour mixture alternately with buttermilk to creamed mixture. Stir in vanilla and nuts. Grease three 9-inch round cake pans and dust with powdered sugar. Divide batter between three pans. Bake at 325 degrees 35 to 45 minutes.

ICING

2½ cups sugar
1 cup evaporated milk
1 stick butter
1 cup marshmallow cream
1 (6-ounce) package semi-sweet chocolate chips
1 cup chopped pecans

Combine sugar and milk in a saucepan. Cook over low heat to soft ball stage. Remove from heat. Add butter, marshmallow cream and chocolate chips. Stir until all have melted and is smooth. Spread icing between cake layers, over top and sides of stacked cake. Top with pecans.

Yield: 12 servings

Fabulous!

Wartime Chocolate Cake

3 cups all-purpose flour
2 cups sugar
6 tablespoons cocoa powder
1 teaspoon salt
2 teaspoons baking soda

12 tablespoons vegetable oil
2 tablespoons vinegar
2 tablespoons vanilla
2 cups cold water

Combine flour, sugar, cocoa, salt and baking soda. In a separate bowl, blend oil, vinegar, vanilla and water. Add to flour mixture. Mix well. Pour batter into a greased and floured 10 cup tube pan. Bake at 350 degrees 45 minutes.

Yield: 10 to 12 servings

This recipe was developed during World War II when dairy products were rationed.

Zucchini Cake

2½ cups all-purpose flour
2 cups sugar
1½ teaspoons cinnamon
1 teaspoon salt
½ teaspoon baking powder
½ teaspoon baking soda

1 cup vegetable oil
4 eggs
2 cups shredded zucchini
½ cup chopped walnuts
(optional)

Combine flour, sugar, cinnamon, salt, baking powder and baking soda. Blend oil and eggs. Add to flour mixture and mix well. Stir in zucchini. Mix thoroughly. Fold in walnuts. Pour batter into a greased and floured 10-inch Bundt pan or 13 x 9 x 2-inch baking dish. Bake at 350 degrees 50 minutes for Bundt or 35 minutes for baking dish. Cool 10 minutes. Remove from pan.

Yield: 10 to 12 servings

Banana Ice Box Cake

2¼ cups all-purpose flour
1½ cups sugar
1½ teaspoons baking powder
1 teaspoon baking soda
½ teaspoon salt
1 cup mashed ripe bananas,
    about 3

¾ cup buttermilk
½ cup vegetable shortening
1 teaspoon vanilla
2 eggs, room temperature
    about 2 hours

Combine flour, sugar, baking powder, baking soda and salt. Add bananas, buttermilk, shortening and vanilla. Beat on low speed until combined. Add eggs and beat 2 minutes. Pour batter into two greased and floured 8-inch or 9-inch round cake pans or one 13 x 9 x 2-inch baking dish. Bake at 350 degrees 25 to 30 minutes for round pans or 30 minutes for baking dish. Cool in pans 10 minutes. Remove to cool completely on wire racks or place baking dish on wire rack. Frost with cream cheese frosting.

Yield: 12 servings

Cream Cheese Frosting

1 (8-ounce) package cream cheese,
    softened
1 stick butter, softened

2 teaspoons vanilla
5¾-6¼ cups sifted powdered
    sugar

Beat cream cheese, butter and vanilla until light and fluffy. Gradually add 2 cups powdered sugar, beating well. Beat in additional powdered sugar to reach spreading consistency. Frost top and sides of two 8 or 9-inch cake layers. Use half frosting recipe for a 13 x 9 x 2-inch cake. Cover and store frosted cake in refrigerator.

Yield: 3 to 4 cups frosting

For Chocolate Cream Cheese Frosting, prepare frosting as above, except beat in ½ cup unsweetened cocoa powder into cream cheese mixture and reduce powdered sugar to 5¼-5¾ cups. Makes 3⅔ cups

Peter Rabbit's Carrot Cake

CAKE

2 cups all-purpose flour
1 teaspoon cinnamon
2 teaspoons baking soda
½ teaspoon salt
4 large eggs
¾ cup packed brown sugar

⅓ cup honey
1 cup corn oil
1 cup chopped walnuts
3½ cups lightly packed grated
carrots

Sift together flour, cinnamon, baking soda and salt. Combine eggs, brown sugar and honey. Beat until light and smooth. Gradually beat in oil. Blend in flour mixture. Stir in walnuts and carrots. Divide batter between two greased and floured 8-inch round cake pans. Bake at 350 degrees 30 to 35 minutes or until tester comes out clean. Cool 5 minutes in pan. Loosen edges and invert onto rack. Reinvert to cool completely.

LEMON CURD AND CREAM CHEESE FILLING AND FROSTING

2 (7-ounce) jars lemon curd
1 cup plus 4 tablespoons cream
cheese, softened

1 tablespoon lemon juice
8 bunny shaped sugar cookies

Beat curd and cream cheese until light and fluffy. Gradually add juice. Spread mixture between cake layers. Spread remaining mixture on top and sides of cake. Press cookies into sides of cake.

Yield: 10 to 12 servings

Adorable, delicious and very festive!

"I never worry about diets. The only carrots
that interest me are the number you get in a diamond."
~ Mae West

Everglades Coconut Layer Cake

CAKE

2½ cups all-purpose flour
1 tablespoon baking powder
1 teaspoon salt
1½ sticks unsalted butter, softened
1½ cups sugar

2 large eggs
3 large egg yolks, reserve whites for frosting
1 teaspoon vanilla
1 cup whole milk

Whisk together flour, baking powder and salt. Set aside. Cream butter and sugar until light and fluffy. Add eggs and egg yolks, one at a time, beating well after each addition. Beat in vanilla. Add flour mixture in three batches alternately with milk, starting and ending with flour. Divide batter between two greased and floured 9-inch round cake pans. Bake at 350 degrees 30 minutes or until tester comes out clean. Cool in pans 10 minutes. Rim edges and invert cakes onto racks. Reinvert and cool completely.

SEVEN MINUTE FROSTING

3 large egg whites
2 teaspoons light corn syrup
½ teaspoon cream of tartar

⅓ cup cold water
1½ cups sugar

Bring 2-inches of water to boil in a saucepan. In a large heatproof bowl, whisk whites, syrup, cream of tartar, cold water and sugar. Place bowl over simmering water, not touching water. Beat with mixer on high speed 7 minutes until stiff peaks form. Remove from heat. Beat 3 to 5 minutes more to cool. Use immediately.

FILLING

¼ cup lemon curd
¾ cup Seven Minute Frosting

1¾ cups sweetened shredded coconut

Whisk together curd and frosting. Place one cake layer on a cake plate. Tuck parchment paper strips under layer. Spread filling over cake. Sprinkle with ½ cup coconut. Place second cake layer on top. Spread 2 cups frosting on top and remaining on sides. Sprinkle remaining coconut over top and pat into sides. Remove paper strips and serve.

Yield: 12 servings

Daffodil Cake

CAKE

1 cup cake flour
¾ cup plus 2 tablespoons sugar
12 egg whites
1½ teaspoons cream of tartar
¼ teaspoon salt

¾ cup sugar
6 egg yolks
1½ teaspoons vanilla
½ teaspoon orange or almond
    extract

Combine flour and sugar and set aside. Beat egg whites, cream of tartar and salt until foamy. Add sugar, 2 tablespoons at a time, beating on high until meringue stiff peaks form. In a separate bowl, beat egg yolks 5 minutes until thickened and lemon colored. Set aside. Gently fold vanilla and orange extract into meringue. Sprinkle flour mixture, ¼ cup at a time, over meringue. Fold in gently until mixture disappears. Pour half meringue into another bowl. Fold in all egg yolks. Spoon yellow and white batters alternately into a 10-inch tube pan. Gently cut through batters to swirl. Bake on the bottom rack at 375 degrees 40 minutes or until top springs back. Invert on funnel and let hang until completely cool. Spread one of the glazes over cake.

LEMON GLAZE

1 cup powdered sugar
½ teaspoon lemon zest
1 teaspoon lemon juice

2 tablespoons milk
1 drop yellow food coloring

Whisk together powdered sugar, zest, juice, milk and food coloring until smooth. The flat part of the cake should be the top. Spread glaze over top of cake and allow to drizzle down the sides.

CREAMY GLAZE

1½ cups powdered sugar
2 tablespoons butter, softened
½ teaspoon orange extract

1-2 tablespoons hot water
1 drop yellow food coloring

Whisk together powdered sugar, butter, extract, water and food coloring. The flat part of the cake should be the top. Spread glaze over top of cake and allow to drizzle down the sides.

Yield: 15 servings

Cousin Robin's Gingerbread Cake

3 cups all-purpose flour
1½ teaspoons cinnamon
1½ teaspoons ground ginger
1 teaspoon baking powder
1 teaspoon baking soda

1 cup vegetable shortening
½ cup packed brown sugar
2 eggs
1 cup molasses

Combine flour, cinnamon, ginger, baking powder and baking soda. In a separate bowl, beat shortening 30 seconds. Add brown sugar and beat until fluffy. Add eggs and molasses and beat 1 minute. Add flour mixture and one cup water alternately until blended. Pour batter into a greased 10-inch Bundt pan or 13 x 9 x 2-inch baking dish. Bake at 350 degrees 50 to 55 minutes for Bundt or 45 minutes for baking dish. Make sure tester comes out clean. Cool 30 minutes and serve with homemade applesauce.

Yield: 12 to 15 servings

Popcorn Cake

2 teaspoons vegetable oil
12 cups popped popcorn, plain,
    unsalted or unbuttered
2 cups M&M's

1 cup lightly salted cocktail peanuts
1 stick unsalted butter
¼ cup vegetable oil
1 (16-ounce) package marshmallows

Grease a 10-inch tube pan with oil. Combine popcorn, candies and peanuts. Melt butter in a saucepan. Add oil and marshmallows. Cook and stir until smooth. Pour mixture over popcorn mixture. Stir to coat. Press mixture down into prepared pan. Cover with foil and let stand 3 to 4 hours. Shake gently and invert cake onto cake plate. Serve at room temperature.

Yield: 12 to 15 servings

It is very tasty, fun to look at and fun to eat for all ages.

Kentucky Glazed Orange Cake

CAKE

2 sticks butter, softened	3 teaspoons baking powder
2 cups sugar	¼ teaspoon salt
5 eggs, room temperature	¾ cup orange juice
3 cups sifted all-purpose flour	Zest of 1 orange

Cream butter until fluffy. Beat in sugar until light. Beat in eggs, one at a time. Sift together flour, baking powder and salt. Add flour mixture alternately with juice to creamed mixture. Stir in zest. Pour batter into a greased and floured 10-inch tube pan. Bake at 350 degrees 1 hour or until tester comes out clean.

GLAZE

2 sticks butter, melted	⅓ cup bourbon whiskey
⅔ cup sugar	

Melt butter in a saucepan. Add sugar and stir until sugar dissolves. Add bourbon. Pour over hot cake in the pan. Cool completely.

Yield: 12 to 15 servings

"Too much of a good thing is wonderful."

~ Mae West

Pineapple Upside Down Cake

1 (8½-ounce) can sliced pineapple
3 tablespoons butter, melted
½ cup packed brown sugar
4 maraschino cherries, halved
5⅓ tablespoons butter, softened
½ cup sugar

1 egg
1 teaspoon vanilla
1 cup sifted all-purpose flour
1¼ teaspoons baking powder
¼ teaspoon salt

Drain pineapple, reserving syrup. Halve pineapple slices. Pour butter in the bottom of an 8 x 8 x 2-inch baking dish. Sprinkle with brown sugar and 1 tablespoon reserve syrup. Add water to remaining syrup to make one-half cup. Arrange pineapple in dish. Place cherry in center of each slice. Cream butter and sugar until light. Beat in egg and vanilla. Sift together flour, baking powder and salt. Add flour mixture alternately with reserved syrup to creamed mixture. Beat well after each addition. Spread batter over pineapple. Bake at 350 degrees 40 to 45 minutes. Cool 5 minutes. Invert onto a serving plate. Serve warm.

Yield: 6 to 8 servings

As little girls, this was one of the first cakes we ever made.

Pumpkin Cake

CAKE

2 cups sifted all-purpose flour
2 teaspoons baking soda
½ teaspoon salt
1 teaspoon ground cloves
2 teaspoons cinnamon
½ teaspoon ground ginger

¼ teaspoon nutmeg
4 eggs, room temperature
2 cups sugar
1 cup vegetable oil
1 (16-ounce) can pumpkin

Sift together flour, baking soda, salt, cloves, cinnamon, ginger and nutmeg. Set aside. Beat in eggs and sugar until light and fluffy. Beat in oil and pumpkin. Blend in flour mixture. Pour batter into a 9-inch tube pan. Bake at 350 degrees 1 hour or until top springs back. Cool in pan. Using a spatula, loosen cake from pan and remove. Place on a cake plate.

CREAM CHEESE FROSTING

2 (3-ounce) packages cream cheese, softened

1 tablespoon rum or vanilla extract
3 cups powdered sugar

Beat cream cheese and rum until smooth. Gradually beat in powdered sugar until light and fluffy. Spread frosting over cake, making swirls with a knife.

Yield: 12 servings

Although you have a choice of extracts, the rum has always been our choice and a hit with family and friends.

Old-Fashioned Blueberry Cake

2 cups all-purpose flour	1 cup milk
1½ cups sugar	2 eggs
2 teaspoons baking powder	1 cup blueberries, fresh or frozen
1 teaspoon salt	¼ cup sugar
1⅓ sticks butter, softened	½ teaspoon cinnamon

Combine flour, sugar, baking powder, salt, butter, milk and eggs. Blend on low speed until moistened. Beat on high 3 minutes. Pour batter into a greased and floured 13 x 9 x 2-inch baking dish. Arrange blueberries on top. Combine sugar and cinnamon. Sprinkle on top. Bake at 350 degrees 40 to 50 minutes or until cake springs back when touched. Cut into squares. Serve warm or cold with whipped cream, ice cream or plain.

Yield: 12 to 15 servings

Kathy has been making this recipe since 1971. It is easy to make and it is Uncle Vinnie's favorite.

"There is one thing more exasperating than a wife who can cook and won't, and that is a wife who can't cook and will."

~ ROBERT FROST

Rhubarb Cake

TOPPING

½ cup sugar   1 teaspoon cinnamon
¼ cup chopped nuts

Combine sugar, nuts and cinnamon. Set aside.

CAKE

½ cup vegetable shortening   ½ teaspoon salt
1½ cups sugar   1 teaspoon baking soda
1 egg   1 cup sour milk
1 teaspoon vanilla   1½ cups diced rhubarb
2 cups all-purpose flour

Cream shortening. Blend in sugar, egg, vanilla. Combine flour, salt and baking soda. Add flour mixture alternately with milk to shortening. Fold in rhubarb. Pour batter into well greased and floured 13 x 9 x 2-inch baking dish. Sprinkle with topping. Bake at 350 degrees 30 minutes.

Yield: 10 to 12 servings

Bourbon Brown Sugar Pound Cake

3 cups all-purpose flour
¾ teaspoon salt
½ teaspoon baking powder
½ teaspoon baking soda
¾ cup milk
2 teaspoons vanilla
4 tablespoons bourbon whiskey
1½ cups packed dark brown sugar

½ cup sugar
2 sticks butter, softened
5 large eggs
2 tablespoons orange juice
⅓ cup sugar
2 tablespoons bourbon whiskey
Strawberries and blueberries for garnish

Combine flour, salt, baking powder and baking soda. In a one cup measuring cup, blend milk, vanilla and bourbon. Cream brown sugar and sugar until free of lumps. Add butter and beat 5 minutes until creamy. Add eggs, one at a time, beating well after each addition. Add flour mixture alternately with milk mixture to creamed mixture, starting and ending with flour. Pour batter into a greased and floured Bundt pan. Bake at 325 degrees 1 hour 15 minutes or until tester comes out clean. Cool in pan on a rack 10 minutes. Remove from pan. Whisk together juice, sugar and bourbon. Drizzle glaze over warm cake. Cool completely. Garnish with berries.

Yield: 24 servings

"A balanced meal in the south is ½ fat and ½ sugar."

~ Aunt Pat

Chocolate Sour Cream Pound Cake

2 sticks butter, softened
2 cups sugar
1 cup packed light brown sugar
6 large eggs
2½ cups all-purpose flour

¼ teaspoon baking soda
½ cup cocoa powder
1 (8-ounce) container sour cream
2 teaspoons vanilla

Beat butter until soft and creamy. Gradually add sugar and brown sugar, beating 5 to 7 minutes. Add eggs, one at a time, beating just until yellow disappears. Combine flour, baking soda and cocoa. Add flour mixture alternately with sour cream to creamed mixture, starting and ending with flour mixture. Mix at low speed after each addition. Stir in vanilla. Pour batter into a greased and floured 10-inch tube pan. Bake at 325 degrees 1 hour, 20 minutes or until tester comes out clean. Cool in pan 15 minutes. Remove from pan and cool completely.

Yield: 12 to 15 servings

Apple-Ginger Cranberry Pie

8 Golden Delicious apples, peeled, cored and thinly sliced
1½ cups cranberries
¼ cup chopped crystallized ginger
1 tablespoon lemon juice

3 tablespoons all-purpose flour
¼ teaspoon salt
¾ cup sugar
Pastry for a 9-inch double crust pie

Combine apples, cranberries, ginger, juice, flour, salt and sugar. Line a 10-inch pie plate with pastry. Pour apple filling into crust. Place second pastry sheet over filling. Seal and flute edges. Cut slits or decorative holes on top. Bake on bottom rack at 400 degrees 45 to 50 minutes or until golden browned and bubbly.

Yield: 8 servings

Perfect Pound Cake

2 cups sugar
2 sticks unsalted butter, melted
4 eggs
4 teaspoons vanilla

3 cups all-purpose flour
2 teaspoons baking powder
1 cup milk

Beat sugar and butter until creamy. Add eggs, one at a time, beating well after each addition. Beat in vanilla. In a separate bowl, combine flour and baking powder. Gradually add flour mixture alternately with milk to creamed mixture, beating on low speed until well mixed. Pour batter into a greased and floured 12-cup Bundt pan. Bake at 350 degrees 50 to 60 minutes or until tester comes out clean. Cool 10 minutes. Remove from pan.

Yield: 16 servings

For an added flair, dust cake slices with powdered sugar. Add dollops of strawberry jam around the dessert plate for an extra taste and a lovely presentation.

March Madness Pie

1 stick butter, melted
1 cup semi-sweet chocolate chips
1 cup chopped pecans
1 teaspoon vanilla
½ cup all-purpose flour

½ cup sugar
½ cup packed brown sugar
2 eggs, beaten
1 (9-inch) pie crust, unbaked

Pour warm butter over chocolate chips and stir until melted. Combine pecans, vanilla, flour, sugar, brown sugar and eggs. Stir into chocolate mixture. Pour filling into pie crust. Bake at 350 degrees 30 to 40 minutes.

Yield: 8 servings

An old Southern tradition.

Blue-Barb Pie

¼ teaspoon salt
1 teaspoon cinnamon
1 cup sugar
¼ cup all-purpose flour

2 cups chopped rhubarb
2 cups blueberries
Pastry for 9-inch double crust pie
1 tablespoon butter

Combine salt, cinnamon, sugar and flour. Add rhubarb and blueberries. Gently mix. Line a 9-inch pie plate with pastry. Pour filling into crust. Dot with butter. Make a lattice top with second pastry. Seal edges. Bake at 450 degrees 10 minutes. Reduce heat to 400 degrees and bake an additional 30 minutes.

Yield: 8 servings

Midge's Rhubarb Meringue Pie

FILLING
1½ cups sugar
6 tablespoons all-purpose flour
5 cups diced young unpeeled
   rhubarb

4 egg yolks
1 (9-inch) pie crust, unbaked

Combine sugar and flour. Stir in rhubarb. Add egg yolks and mix well. Pour filling into pie shell. Bake at 425 degrees 1 hour until rhubarb is tender. Cool 5 to 10 minutes.

MERINGUE
4 egg whites
½ teaspoon cream of tartar

½ cup sugar

Beat egg whites with cream of tartar until frothy. Gradually beat in sugar until stiff and glossy. Pile meringue on pie being careful to seal meringue to pie crust. Bake at 400 degrees 8 to 10 minutes or until browned.

Yield: 8 to 10 servings

Apple Pie

¾ cup sugar
2 tablespoons all-purpose flour
1 teaspoon cinnamon
Dash of ground nutmeg

6-8 tart apples, peeled, cored and thinly sliced
Pastry for 9-inch double crust pie
3 tablespoons butter
Lemon zest

Combine sugar, flour, cinnamon and nutmeg. Add apples and toss to coat. Line a 9-inch pie plate with pastry. Pour filling into crust. Dot with butter and sprinkle with zest. Place top pastry over filling and press edges to seal. Cut slits in top for steam to escape. Bake at 400 degrees 50 minutes or until done.

Yield: 8 servings

Serve warm with vanilla ice cream.

Buttermilk Pie

1¼ cups sugar
3 tablespoons all-purpose flour
4 eggs, slightly beaten
1 stick butter, melted and cooled
1 cup buttermilk

Zest of 1 lemon
1 tablespoon lemon juice
1 teaspoon vanilla
⅛ teaspoon ground nutmeg
Pastry for a 9-inch single crust pie

Combine sugar and flour. Add eggs and mix well. Stir in butter and buttermilk. Add zest, juice, vanilla and nutmeg. Mix well. Line a 9-inch pie plate with pastry. Pour filling into crust. Bake at 425 degrees 15 minutes. Reduce heat to 350 degrees and bake an additional 40 minutes or until set. Serve at room temperature.

Yield: 8 servings

If you have any extra pastry, you may cut out designs and adhere them to the crust with cold water.

Cousin Catherine's Cranberry Pie

1½ cups cranberries
½ cup water
¾ cup sugar

⅛ teaspoon salt
Pastry for an 8-inch double
  crust pie

Sort cranberries. Rinse and cook in a covered saucepan with water until skins burst. Stir in sugar and salt. Cool filling. Line an 8-inch pie plate with pastry. Pour in filling. Place pastry strips on top to form a lattice crust. Secure edges with a strip of pastry and brush with water. Bake at 350 degrees 45 to 50 minutes until browned.

Yield: 8 servings

Peach Blackberry Pie

4 peaches, peeled and sliced
2 cups blackberries
⅔ cup sugar
3½ tablespoons quick cooking
  tapioca

1 tablespoon unsalted butter, cut
  into small pieces
Pastry for a 9-inch double
  crust pie

Combine peaches, blackberries, sugar and tapioca. Toss to coat. Line a 9-inch pie plate with pastry. Pour filling into crust. Dot with butter. Make a lattice top with second pastry. Bake at 400 degrees 40 minutes or until fruit is bubbly and crust golden browned.

Yield: 8 servings

What a wonderful recipe to make during August when fresh peaches can be picked at your local orchard.

Blueberry Pie

4 cups blueberries, fresh or frozen
¾ cup sugar
3 tablespoons all-purpose flour
½ teaspoon lemon zest

1 teaspoon cinnamon
Pastry for 9-inch double
  pie crust
1 tablespoon butter

Combine blueberries, sugar, flour and cinnamon. Line a 9-inch pie plate with pastry. Pour filling into crust. Dot with butter and sprinkle with zest. Top with second pastry and seal edges. Cut slits in top crust. Bake at 400 degrees 35 to 40 minutes.

Yield: 8 servings

Old-Fashioned Blueberry Pie

4 cups blueberries
1 cup maple syrup
¼ cup all-purpose flour

¼ cup quick cooking tapioca
4 teaspoons lemon juice
Pastry for a 9-inch double crust pie

Combine blueberries, syrup, flour, tapioca and juice. Let stand 15 minutes. Line a 9-inch pie plate with pastry sheet. Pour filling into crust. Make a lattice top with second pastry. Bake at 400 degrees 35 to 40 minutes.

Yield: 8 servings

Raspberry Pie

4 cups raspberries
¾ cup sugar
3 tablespoons all-purpose flour
¼ teaspoon dried lemon zest

½ teaspoon cinnamon
Pastry for a 9-inch double crust pie
1 tablespoon butter, cut into small
  pieces

Combine raspberries, sugar, flour, zest and cinnamon. Gently toss to coat. Line a 9-inch pie plate with pastry. Pour filling into crust. Dot with butter pieces. Top with lattice pastry and seal edges. Bake at 400 degrees 35 to 40 minutes.

Yield: 8 servings

Perfect Peach Pie

BUTTERMILK CRUST

2½ cups all-purpose flour
5 teaspoons sugar
½ teaspoon salt

6 tablespoons unsalted butter, cut into ½-inch pieces
¼ cup vegetable shortening, cut into ½-inch pieces
¾ cup buttermilk

Blend flour, sugar and salt in a food processor. Add butter and shortening. Pulse on /off 25 times until crumbly. Blend in buttermilk with on/off until moist clumps form. Add more buttermilk if too dry. Gather dough into a ball. Divide into two pieces, one slightly larger than the other. Flatten into a disc. Wrap in plastic wrap and refrigerate 1 hour or overnight.

PEACH FILLING

¾ cup sugar
¼ cup all-purpose flour
1½ teaspoons lemon juice
½ teaspoon cinnamon
¼ teaspoon ground cardamom

3¾-4 pounds ripe peaches
2 tablespoons unsalted butter, cut into small pieces
1 egg, beaten
1 tablespoon sugar

Combine sugar, flour, juice, cinnamon and cardamom. Cook peaches in boiling water 30 seconds. Transfer to a bowl of cold water. Cool. Peel, halve and pit peaches. Slice peaches and add to sugar mixture. Toss to coat. Let peaches stand 20 minutes, stirring often. Roll out large dough disc on a floured surface to a 12 to13-inch round. Line a 9-inch glass pie plate with dough. Trim overhang to ¾ inches. Pour filling into crust. Dot with butter. Roll out second disc to a 12-inch round. Drape pastry over filling. Pinch overhang and edges of crust together. Crimp edges. Cut several slits in top. Brush pastry with egg. Sprinkle with sugar. Bake at 400 degrees 50 minutes or until browned and juice is bubbly. Cool on rack 1 hour. Serve warm or room temperature.

Yield: 8 servings

Strawberry Pie

1½ quarts strawberries, rinsed
  and hulled
1 cup sugar
3 tablespoons cornstarch

2 tablespoons lemon juice
1 (9-inch) pie crust, baked
Whipped cream

Mash half strawberries in a saucepan. Combine sugar and cornstarch. Add to strawberries. Cook and stir 5 minutes until thickened and clear. Stir in juice. Cool. Add remaining strawberries, saving 4 to 5 for garnish. Pour filling into crust. Refrigerate. Top with whipped cream and garnish with strawberries.

Yield: 8 servings

Strawberry-Rhubarb Pie

1 pound rhubarb, cut into
  ½-inch pieces
1 cup sliced strawberries
1½ cups sugar

3 tablespoons quick cooking
  tapioca
1 teaspoon cinnamon
Pastry for a 9-inch double crust pie
1 tablespoon butter

Combine rhubarb, strawberries, sugar, tapioca and cinnamon. Let stand 20 minutes. Line a 9-inch pie plate with pastry. Pour filling into crust. Dot with butter. Make a lattice top crust. Seal edges. Bake at 400 degrees 35 to 40 minutes.

Yield: 8 servings

Over the years, we have discovered that when asked what is one's favorite pie, the answer is Strawberry Rhubarb.

Custard Pecan Pie

1 stick butter	¼ teaspoon salt
2 cups sugar	1 cup buttermilk
2 teaspoons vanilla	½ cup chopped pecans
3 eggs	1 (9-inch) pie crust, unbaked
3 tablespoons all-purpose flour	

Cream butter and sugar, adding sugar one-half cup at a time. Stir in vanilla. Add eggs, one at a time. Combine flour and salt. Gradually blend into creamed mixture. Stir in buttermilk. Sprinkle pecans in bottom of pie crust. Pour custard over pecans. Bake at 300 degrees 1 hour, 30 minutes. Serve at room temperature.

Yield: 8 servings

Maple Walnut Pie

Pastry for 9-inch deep dish crust pie	¼ teaspoon cinnamon
2½ cups chopped walnuts	5 tablespoons butter, melted
1 cup dark maple syrup	½ teaspoon vanilla
5 eggs	½ teaspoon salt
2 teaspoons lemon juice	

Line a 9-inch deep dish with pastry. Spread walnuts in pie crust. Whisk together syrup, eggs, juice, cinnamon, butter, vanilla and salt until smooth. Pour filling into crust. Bake at 375 degrees 35 to 40 minutes.

Yield: 8 servings

Best when served with vanilla ice cream or whipped cream.

Date Nut Pumpkin Pie

CRUST

1½ cups all-purpose flour
½ teaspoon salt

½ cup vegetable shortening
4-5 tablespoons cold water

Combine flour and salt. Cut in shortening with a pastry blender. Stir in water, one tablespoon at a time, until dough forms a ball. Wrap in plastic wrap and refrigerate.

DATE-NUT LAYER

1 (8-ounce) package pitted dates, chopped
¾ cup water
⅓ cup packed brown sugar

4 tablespoons butter
½ cup chopped walnuts
½ teaspoon cinnamon

Combine dates and water in a 2-quart saucepan. Bring to boil. Reduce heat and cook until dates are soft, stirring constantly. Add brown sugar and butter. Mix well. Remove from heat. Stir in walnuts and cinnamon. Cool.

PUMPKIN FILLING

2 large eggs
1 (16-ounce) can solid pack pumpkin
1 cup evaporated milk
½ cup sugar
½ cup packed brown sugar

½ teaspoon cinnamon
½ teaspoon ground ginger
½ teaspoon ground nutmeg
¼ teaspoon salt
⅛ teaspoon ground cloves

Blend eggs and pumpkin. Stir in milk, sugar, brown sugar, cinnamon, ginger, nutmeg, salt and cloves. Roll three-fourths dough on a lightly floured surface. Line a 9-inch pie plate. Trim edges and reserve. Pour date-nut mixture into crust. Spread pumpkin filling on top. Roll remaining dough to ⅛-inch thick. Cut out 3-inch pumpkin designs and a few leaves. Arrange on filling. Cut out small leaves with a small knife. Moisten pie crust with water. Press small leaves around edge of pie. Bake at 450 degrees 10 minutes. Reduce heat to 350 degrees and bake an additional 35 minutes. Cool and serve.

Yield: 10 servings

Although this recipe appears to be difficult, it really is not. It is truly worth the effort. This was the first pie Nancy ever made by herself.

Banbury Turnovers

1 cup sugar
1 tablespoon all-purpose flour
1 egg
1 cup seedless raisins

¼ cup chopped walnuts
Zest of 1 lemon
Juice of 1 lemon
Pastry dough

Combine sugar and flour. Stir in egg. Add raisins, nuts, zest and juice. Roll out dough to ⅛-inch thickness. Cut into squares or circles about 4-inches across. Place 2 teaspoons filling on dough pieces. Moisten dough edges with water. Fold over filling, pressing edges to seal. Bake at 400 degrees until browned.

Yield: 6 to 8 servings

For leftover crust or freshly made pie crust. Here is another old recipe from Cousin Catherine! Great when served with tea during the holidays.

Savannah Peach Cobbler

2 cups sliced peaches
½ cup sugar
1 stick unsalted butter
¾ cup all-purpose flour

2 teaspoons baking powder
1 cup sugar
¼ teaspoon salt
¾ cup milk

Combine peaches and sugar. Set aside. Preheat oven to 350 degrees. Place butter in bottom of deep baking dish. Place in oven until butter melts. Mix together flour, baking powder, sugar, salt and milk until well blended. Pour batter over butter. Do not stir. Arrange sugared peaches over batter. Do not stir. Bake 40 to 45 minutes or until lightly browned and puffy.

Yield: 8 servings

Fruit Cobblers

BISCUIT TOPPING

1 cup all-purpose flour
2 tablespoons sugar
1½ teaspoons baking powder
¼ teaspoon salt

4 tablespoons butter,
   softened
¼ cup milk
1 egg, slightly beaten

Combine flour, sugar, baking powder and salt. Cut in butter. Blend milk and egg. Add to flour mixture until moistened. Set aside.

RHUBARB COBBLER

1 cup sugar
2 tablespoons cornstarch
½ teaspoon cinnamon
1 tablespoon water

1 tablespoon butter
4 cups rhubarb, cut into 1-inch
   pieces or 3 cups rhubarb
   and 1 cup strawberries

Combine sugar, cornstarch, cinnamon, water, butter and rhubarb. Bring to boil. Cook and stir 1 minute. Pour filling into an 8-inch round baking dish. Immediately, spoon biscuit topping in six mounds. Bake at 400 degrees 20 to 25 minutes. Serve warm with whipped cream or vanilla ice cream.

PEACH COBBLER

1½ teaspoons cornstarch
¼ teaspoon ground mace
½ cup packed brown sugar
½ cup water

4 cups sliced peaches
1 tablespoon lemon juice
1 tablespoon butter

Combine cornstarch, mace, brown sugar and water. Cook and stir until thickened. Add peaches, juice and butter. Cook 5 minutes until hot. Pour filling into an 8-inch round baking dish. Immediately spoon biscuit topping in six mounds. Bake at 400 degrees 20 to 25 minutes. Serve warm with whipped cream or ice cream.

Yield: 6 servings

Maine Blueberry Gingerbread

½ cup vegetable shortening
1 cup sugar
1 egg
2 cups sifted all-purpose flour
½ teaspoon ginger
1 teaspoon cinnamon

½ teaspoon salt
1 cup sour milk or buttermilk
1 teaspoon baking soda
3 tablespoons molasses
1 cup blueberries, fresh or frozen
3 tablespoons sugar

Cream shortening and sugar. Add egg and mix well. Sift together flour, ginger, cinnamon and salt. Blend milk and baking soda. Add flour mixture alternately with milk to creamed mixture. Add molasses. Fold in blueberries. Pour batter into a greased and floured 9 x 9 x 2-inch baking dish. Sprinkle with sugar. Bake at 350 degrees 50 minutes to 1 hour.

Yield: 9 to 12 servings

Summer Blackberry Crisp

TOPPING
1 cup all-purpose flour
1 cup sugar

1 teaspoon baking powder
1 egg

Combine flour, sugar and baking powder. Make a well in the center. Add egg and blend until crumbly. Set aside.

FILLING
2 tablespoons all-purpose flour
¾ cup sugar

4-5 cups blackberries
1 stick unsalted butter, melted

Combine flour and sugar. Sprinkle over blackberries and gently toss to coat. Pour filling into a well-buttered 9 x 9 x 2-inch baking dish. Sprinkle with topping. Drizzle butter over topping. Place dish on a baking sheet. Bake at 375 degrees 45 minutes.

Yield: 6 servings

Meringue Nests with Blackberries

6 egg whites
⅛ teaspoon salt
1½ teaspoons cream of tartar
1 teaspoon vanilla

1½ cups sugar
4 cups blackberries
2 tablespoons sugar

Beat egg whites, salt and cream of tartar until soft peaks form. Add vanilla. Gradually add sugar, 3 tablespoons at a time, beating well after each addition until stiff. Line a baking sheet with parchment paper. Scoop out ¾ cup batter and drop onto paper, making 3-inch wide mound. With the back of a spoon, make a shallow well in the center of the mound. Bake at 250 degrees 1 hour. Turn off oven and cool meringues in oven 2 hours or overnight. Slip meringues into a paper bag in a single layer and store in a dry place until ready to use, up to 3 to 4 days. Combine blackberries and sugar. Mash some of the blackberries. Cover and refrigerate for several hours. When ready to serve. Places nest on individual plates. Spoon blackberry filling and juice over each.

Yield: 8 to 10 servings

"Never forget your summertimes, my dears."
~ STUART LITTLE

Blueberry Cake with Crumb Topping

TOPPING

½ cup sugar
⅓ cup all-purpose flour

1 teaspoon cinnamon
4 tablespoons butter, softened

Combine sugar, flour and cinnamon. Cut in butter until crumbly. Set aside.

CAKE

¾ cup sugar
1 stick butter
1 egg
½ cup milk

2 cups all-purpose flour
½ teaspoon salt
2 teaspoons baking powder
2 cups blueberries

Cream sugar and butter. Blend together egg and milk. Sift together flour, salt and baking powder. Add flour mixture alternately with milk mixture to creamed mixture. Fold in blueberries. Pour batter into a greased 9 x 9 x 2-inch baking dish. Sprinkle topping over batter. Bake at 375 degrees 30 to 40 minutes.

Yield: 6 to 8 servings

Blueberry Coffee Cake

TOPPING

¼ cup sugar
1 teaspoon cinnamon

1 teaspoon vanilla

Combine sugar, cinnamon and vanilla. Set aside.

CAKE

1 stick butter, softened
1 cup sugar
2 eggs
1 cup sour cream

2 cups all-purpose flour
1 teaspoon baking soda
1 teaspoon baking powder
2 cups frozen blueberries, slightly
thawed

Cream butter and sugar. Add eggs and sour cream. Blend in flour, baking soda and baking powder. Mix 1 minute. Fold in blueberries. Pour batter into a greased and floured 10-inch Bundt pan. Sprinkle with topping. Bake at 350 degrees 55 to 60 minutes.

Yield: 10 to 12 servings

Swedish Almond Coffee Cake

4 eggs
2 cups all-purpose flour
2 cups sugar
2 teaspoons almond extract

2 sticks butter, melted
Sugar for topping
1 cup chopped walnuts

Beat eggs until fluffy. Add flour, sugar and extract. Mix well. Stir in butter. Pour batter into a greased 13 x 9 x 2-inch baking dish. Sprinkle with sugar and nuts. Bake at 350 degrees 35 to 40 minutes or until tester comes out clean.

Yield: 10 to 12 servings

Blueberry Rhubarb Crumble

1½ cups rolled oats	2 cups rhubarb, cut into
⅔ cup packed brown sugar	1-inch pieces
½ cup all-purpose flour	½ cup sugar
1 stick butter	2 tablespoons all-purpose
3 cups blueberries	flour

Combine oats, brown sugar and flour. Cut in butter until crumbly. Reserve ⅔ cup crumb mixture. Pat remaining mixture into the bottom of a greased 9 x 2-inch round baking pan. Bake at 350 degrees 10 to 15 minutes or until lightly browned. Combine blueberries and rhubarb. Add sugar and flour and toss to coat. Spoon fruit over crust. Sprinkle reserved crumb mixture on top. Bake an additional 45 to 50 minutes.

Yield: 6 servings

Warm from the oven fruit desserts are old time favorites. Serve with whipped cream or light cream.

Spanish Custard Flan De Leche

1 cup sugar	¼ teaspoon anise extract
½ cup water	1 teaspoon vanilla
6 eggs	Pinch salt
2 cups sugar	2 cups boiling milk

Combine sugar and water. Bring to boil. Reduce heat and stir until dark brown. Divide into six custard cups. Beat eggs. Add sugar, anise, vanilla and salt. Beat until smooth. Gradually stir in milk. Strain with a fine sieve or cheesecloth. Pour mixture into custard cups. Place cups in a large shallow pan. Add hot water to a depth of 1-inch. Bake at 350 degrees 30 minutes. Do not let water boil. Cool in the refrigerator. When ready to serve, press edges of the custard with a spoon to break away from the cup. Invert onto a dessert plate. The caramel tops the custard.

Yield: 6 servings

Gingerbread with Lemon Orange Glaze

GLAZE

⅔ cup powdered sugar   2 tablespoons orange juice
2 tablespoons lemon juice

Sift sugar into a bowl. Add juices and mix well.

CAKE

1⅔ cups all-purpose flour   1 egg, beaten
1¼ teaspoons baking soda   ½ cup sugar
¾ teaspoon ground ginger   ½ cup molasses
¾ teaspoon cinnamon   ½ cup boiling water
½ teaspoon salt   ½ cup vegetable oil
¼ teaspoon ground cloves

Sift together flour, baking soda, ginger, cinnamon, salt and cloves. Add egg, sugar and molasses. Mix well. Stir in water and oil until smooth. Pour batter into a greased 9 x 9 x 2-inch baking dish. Bake at 350 degrees 35 to 40 minutes. Pour glaze over top while gingerbread is hot. Cool in pan.

Yield: 6 servings

Pumpkin Maple Custard

1 cup canned pumpkin	1 cup heavy cream
½ cup maple syrup	1 teaspoon ground ginger
¼ cup sugar	Pinch of nutmeg
4 large eggs, slightly beaten	Whipped cream

Whisk together pumpkin, maple syrup, sugar, eggs, cream, ginger and nutmeg until well combined. Pour ¾ cup mixture into six ramekins or custard cups. Set ramekins in a water bath. Bake at 325 degrees 25 to 30 minutes or until edges are firm and center is slightly moist. Serve warm with whipped cream and drizzle top with maple syrup.

Yield: 6 servings

Blueberry Pudding

3 cups blueberries	2 teaspoons baking powder
1 cup packed brown sugar	½ teaspoon salt
6 tablespoons butter	2 teaspoons orange zest
1 cup sugar	¾ cup orange juice
1⅓ sticks butter, softened	2 cups heavy cream
Dash of vanilla	6 tablespoons Grand Marnier™
2 eggs	(optional)
1½ cups all-purpose flour	

Combine blueberries, brown sugar and butter in a saucepan. Simmer over low heat. Cream sugar, butter and vanilla. Beat in eggs. Sift together flour, baking powder and salt. Add to creamed mixture. Stir in zest and juice. Pour blueberries into the bottom of a 3-quart baking dish. Pour batter over berries. Bake at 350 degrees 45 minutes. Whip cream and stir in Grand Marnier™. Serve as a topping.

Yield: 10 to 12 servings

This is a very old recipe. Pudding is an old-fashioned favorite dessert.

Blueberry Summer Pudding

3½ cups blueberries
¾ cup sugar
2 teaspoons orange juice

3 tablespoons butter, softened
6-9 slices firm white sandwich
   bread, crust removed

Line an 8-inch loaf pan with plastic wrap. Combine blueberries, sugar and juice. Cook over medium heat. Bring to boil. Cook 5 minutes until berries release their juices. Cool. Spread butter on one side of each slice of bread. Place a layer of bread, buttered side down, in loaf pan. Trim to fit. Spoon half of fruit over bread. Repeat layers of bread and fruit, finishing with bread. Cover with plastic wrap. Refrigerate 8 to 24 hours. Remove top wrap and run a knife between bottom wrap and pan. Invert to a platter. Remove wrap. Use a serrated knife and cut into thick pieces.

Yield: 6 to 8 servings

Chocolate Bread Pudding

9 slices white sandwich bread
3 cups scalded milk
3 eggs
Dash of salt

½ cup sugar
1 teaspoon vanilla
2 (1-ounce) squares semi-sweet
   chocolate, melted and cooled

Trim crust from bread and cut into cubes. Place bread in milk and let stand 15 to 20 minutes. Beat eggs, salt and sugar until smooth. Add vanilla. Beat in chocolate. Stir bread into chocolate mixture. Pour mixture into a 3-quart baking dish. Set dish in a pan of water. Bake at 350 degrees 1 hour, stirring every 20 minutes. Serve with vanilla ice cream.

Yield: 6 to 8 servings

Kathy's Favorite Rice Pudding

½ cup short-grain rice   ¼ cup sugar
½ cup water   1 teaspoon vanilla
3 cups milk   Cinnamon for garnish

Combine rice, water and milk. Bring to boil. Boil 25 to 30 minutes, stirring constantly until rice has absorbed liquid. Stir in sugar and vanilla. Cook 5 minutes more. Divide into individual dessert dishes. Cool. Sprinkle with cinnamon.

Yield: 4 to 6 servings

In Armenian, this is called Gatnabour.

Maple Pudding Cake

1 cup maple syrup   1½ cups all-purpose flour
2 teaspoons vegetable oil   2 teaspoons baking powder
¾ cup sugar   ¼ teaspoon salt
1 egg   1 cup heavy cream
1 cup milk

Pour syrup into a buttered 8 x 8 x 2-inch baking dish. Combine oil, sugar and egg. Stir in milk. Blend flour, baking powder and salt. Add to milk mixture. Mix well. Pour batter over syrup. Top with cream. Bake at 350 degrees 30 minutes.

Yield: 6 to 8 servings

This recipe can be savored during Maple Sugar Time, commonly thought of in New England as the fifth season of the year. This season occurs from late winter into early spring.

Rhubarb Tapioca Pudding

2 cups rhubarb, cut into
   1-inch pieces
1 cup hot water

¾ cup sugar or ½ cup honey
¼ cup quick cooking tapioca
Plain or whipped cream for garnish

Combine rhubarb, water, sugar and tapioca in the top of a double boiler. Cook 25 minutes until rhubarb is tender. Cool and serve with plain or whipped cream.

Yield: 4 to 6 servings

Traditional Indian Pudding

3 cups milk
¾ cup maple syrup
2 tablespoons butter
⅔ cup ground cornmeal

1 teaspoon ground ginger
½ teaspoon ground nutmeg
1½ cups dark seedless raisins
1 cup milk

Combine milk and syrup in a 2-quart saucepan. Heat just until boiling. Add butter. Combine cornmeal, ginger and nutmeg. Gradually stir cornmeal mixture into hot milk. Reduce heat. Cook and stir 10 minutes until thickened. Stir in raisins. Spoon mixture into a buttered 2-quart baking dish. Pour milk on top but do not stir. Bake at 300 degrees 2 hour, 30 minutes until milk is absorbed and top is golden browned.

Yield: 8 servings

Indian pudding was a favorite of our dear father's.

Rhubarb Gelatin

2 quarts chopped rhubarb, 8 cups
½ cup water

2 (3-ounce) packages red gelatin
1½ cups sugar

Cook rhubarb in water until soft. Stir in gelatin and sugar. Mix well. Cool and serve.

Yield: 8 to 10 servings

Our Aunt Pat gave us this old Vermont recipe! You may use strawberry, cherry or cranberry gelatin. It is actually addicting!

Date Pudding

2½ cups chopped dates
2 teaspoons baking soda
2 sticks unsalted butter, softened
   and cut into small pieces
½ cup sugar
4 eggs

2½ cups all-purpose flour
2 teaspoons salt
1 tablespoon vanilla
1 heaping tablespoon baking
   powder
Caramel sauce

Preheat oven to 350 degrees. Place dates in a saucepan and cover with water. Bring to boil. Reduce heat and simmer 3 minutes. Stir in baking soda and cool. Strain dates reserving 1 cup cooking liquid. Cream butter and sugar. Add eggs, one at a time, beating well after each addition. Stir in flour, salt, vanilla and mix well. Add baking powder and reserved cooking liquid. Stir in dates. Pour pudding into a buttered 8 x 8 x 2-inch baking dish. Bake 40 minutes or until golden browned. Cut into squares and serve warm. Pour caramel sauce on individual plates. Place warm pudding over caramel. Drizzle with additional caramel sauce.

Yield: 8 servings

Blondes Have More Fun Toffee Blondies

1 stick unsalted butter, melted
1 cup packed light brown sugar
2 large eggs
1 teaspoon vanilla

¼ teaspoon salt
1½ cups all-purpose flour
1 cup toffee bits

Line the bottom and sides of an 8-inch baking pan with foil, with a bit of overhang. Cream butter and sugar until smooth. Beat in eggs, vanilla and salt. Gradually add flour and mix well. Stir in toffee by hand. Spread batter into prepared pan. Bake at 350 degrees 30 to 35 minutes or until tester comes out clean. Cool completely in pan. Grasp foil and lift blondies from pan. Peel off foil. Cut into squares with a serrated knife.

Yield: 6 to 8 servings

Gentlemen Prefer Blondies

1¼ cups all-purpose flour
½ cup sugar
½ cup packed brown sugar
6 tablespoons butter, softened
1¼ teaspoons baking powder
½ teaspoon salt

1½ teaspoons vanilla
2 large eggs
½ cup semi-sweet chocolate chips
1 (7-ounce) jar macadamia nuts,
   coarsely chopped

Combine flour, sugar, brown sugar, butter, baking powder, salt, vanilla, eggs, chocolate chips and half the nuts. Beat until well blended. Spread batter into a greased 9 x 9 x 2-inch metal baking dish. Top with remaining nuts. Bake at 350 degrees 35 minutes. Cool in pan on a rack. Cut into squares and serve.

Yield: 6 to 8 servings

Gold Brick Brownies

4 (1-ounce) squares unsweetened
  baking chocolate
1½ sticks butter
2 cups sugar
4 eggs
1 cup all-purpose flour

1 cup chopped pecans or walnuts
1 (14-ounce) package caramels,
  unwrapped
2 tablespoons milk
1 cup semi-sweet chocolate chunks

Place chocolate squares and butter in microwave bowl. Microwave on high 2 minutes or until butter is melted. Stir until chocolate is melted. Blend in sugar. Mix in eggs. Add flour and pecans. Mix well. Spread into a 13 x 9 x 2-inch baking dish lined with greased foil. Bake at 350 degrees 30 to 35 minutes. Do not overbake. Combine caramels and milk in a microwave bowl. Microwave on high 2½ minutes, stirring after 1 minute. Stir until caramels are blended. Gently spread over brownie. Sprinkle with chocolate chunks. Cool in pan on a rack. Lift out of pan to a cutting board. Cut into squares.

Yield: 2 dozen brownies

Cranberry Brownies

1 cup sugar
½ cup vegetable oil
2 eggs
2 teaspoons vanilla
½ cup all-purpose flour

½ cup unsweetened cocoa powder
1 teaspoon baking powder
1 cup coarsely chopped fresh or
  frozen cranberries

Beat sugar, oil, eggs and vanilla until smooth. Add flour, cocoa and baking powder. Beat on low speed 1 minute. Add cranberries and mix well. Spread batter into a greased and floured 8 x 8 x 2-inch baking dish. Bake at 350 degrees 25 minutes or until tester comes out clean. Cool completely before cutting.

Yield: 6 servings

George Washington's Cherry Brownies

1½ sticks butter
6 (1-ounce) unsweetened chocolate
  baking squares, chopped
2½ cups sugar
4 eggs
1 egg yolk
1½ teaspoons vanilla

½ teaspoon almond extract
1 cup plus 2 tablespoons
  all-purpose flour
1 teaspoon cinnamon
1 cup dried cherries, halved
1 cup semi-sweet chocolate
  chips

Melt butter and chocolate in a heavy saucepan, stirring until smooth. Remove from heat and stir in sugar. Add eggs, one at a time. Add egg yolk and mix well. Stir in vanilla, almond extract, flour and cinnamon. Add cherries and chocolate chips. Spread batter into a buttered and floured 13 x 9 x 2-inch baking dish. Bake at 350 degrees 35 minutes or until tester comes out clean. Cool in pan on a rack. Cut into 16 or 32 squares.

Yield: 16 servings

Palm Beach Citrus Brownies

BATTER

1½ cups all-purpose flour	4 eggs
2 cups sugar	2 teaspoons orange extract
1 teaspoon salt	1 teaspoon orange zest
2 sticks butter, softened	

Combine flour, sugar and salt. Beat in butter, eggs, extract and zest until blended. Pour batter into a greased 13 x 9 x 2-inch baking dish. Bake at 350 degrees 30 minutes until golden browned. Remove from oven and pierce top of cake with a fork.

GLAZE

1 cup powdered sugar	1 teaspoon orange zest
2 tablespoons orange juice	

Combine powdered sugar, juice and zest until smooth. Pour glaze over warm cake. Cool and cut into squares.

Yield: 24 squares

Kit's Pie Crust

2 cups sifted all-purpose flour	⅔ cup vegetable shortening
1 teaspoon salt	5-7 tablespoons ice water

Sift together flour and salt. Cut in shortening with a pastry blender until crumbly. Sprinkle water over mixture. Gently toss with a fork. Form dough into a ball. Cut ball in half for double crust or lattice top pies.

Yield: 1 double crust pie

For one single crust pie, use 1½ cups flour, ½ teaspoon salt, ½ cup shortening and 4-5 tablespoons ice water.

Hoist the Flag Brownies

1 stick butter, softened	1 cup chopped pecans
1 cup sugar	½ teaspoon almond extract
4 eggs	4 tablespoons butter, softened
1 cup all-purpose flour	2 cups sifted powdered sugar
¼ teaspoon salt	2½ tablespoons green crème
1 (16-ounce) can chocolate syrup	de menthe

Cream butter. Gradually beat in sugar. Add eggs, one at a time, beating well after each addition. In a separate bowl, combine flour and salt. Add flour mixture alternately with chocolate syrup to creamed mixture, beginning and ending with flour mixture. Stir in pecans and almond extract. Spread batter into a greased and floured 13 x 9 x 2-inch baking dish. Bake at 350 degrees 30 minutes or until tester comes out clean. Cool in pan. Beat butter, powdered sugar and crème de menthe until smooth. Spread frosting over brownies. Cool and refrigerate 1 hour. Cut into 1½-inch squares.

Yield: 48 brownies

Hoist the Flag was a favorite to win the Kentucky Derby and everyone looked forward to a Triple Crown sweep. Unfortunately, he was injured and was retired before the Derby.

Raspberry Crumb Bars

2 sticks butter, softened
2 cups all-purpose flour
½ cup firmly packed light brown
   sugar

¼ teaspoon salt
1 (12-ounce) jar seedless red
   raspberry jam

Beat butter on medium speed until creamy. Add flour, brown sugar and salt. Beat until crumbly. Using floured fingers, press 1¾ cups crumb mixture into bottom of 13 x 9 x 2-inch baking dish. Bake at 350 degrees 10 to 12 minutes until browned. Spread jam over baked crust. Top with remaining crumb mixture. Bake 25 to 30 minutes.

Yield: 24 squares

May substitute peach, fig or strawberry rhubarb preserves for raspberry jam.

Raspberries and Blackberries with Ricotta

1 pint red raspberries
1 pint blackberries
2 cups whole milk ricotta cheese

¼ cup powdered sugar
3 tablespoons Amaretto or
   Grand Marnier™

Combine raspberries and blackberries in a shallow serving dish. Drain excess liquid off ricotta. Purée ricotta in a food processor until smooth. Add powdered sugar and Amaretto. Blend well. Spoon cheese into pretty serving dish and refrigerate. To serve, scoop spoonfuls of ricotta cream into footed dessert dishes. Top with fresh berries.

Yield: 8 servings

Childhood Devil Dogs

DOUGH

1 stick butter, softened	1 teaspoon vanilla
1 cup sugar	½ cup cocoa powder
1 egg	1 cup milk
2 cups all-purpose flour	½ teaspoon salt
½ teaspoon baking powder	1½ teaspoons baking soda

Combine butter, sugar and egg. Beat until smooth. Add flour, baking powder, vanilla, cocoa powder, milk, salt and baking soda. Mix until smooth. Drop by rounded tablespoons on a greased baking sheet. Bake at 400 degrees 7 minutes.

FILLING

½ cup vegetable shortening	1 teaspoon vanilla
2 cups powdered sugar	3-4 teaspoons milk
½ small jar marshmallow creme	

Combine shortening, powdered sugar, marshmallow creme, vanilla and milk. Add enough milk to make light and easy to spread. Spread marshmallow filling between two cookies to make sandwiches.

Yield: 8 servings

Our mother would make these delicious treats and wrap each one individually in wax paper. She would place them in the refrigerator. There they would await our arrival from school. Those were the days of homemade 3:00 snacks!

Since we love pink, sometimes we substitute strawberry marshmallow creme for the traditional marshmallow creme.

Notes

_____

_____

_____

_____

_____

_____

_____

_____

_____

_____

_____

_____

_____

_____

Cookies & Candy

*"Anyone who uses the phrase 'easy as taking candy from a baby'
has never tried taking candy from a baby."*

~ UNKNOWN

Black and White Cookies

1¼ cups all-purpose flour
½ teaspoon baking soda
½ teaspoon salt
6 tablespoons unsalted butter,
  softened
½ cup sugar
1 large egg
½ teaspoon vanilla
⅓ cup buttermilk

2 cups powdered sugar
1 tablespoon plus 1 teaspoon
  light corn syrup
2½ teaspoons lemon juice
¼ teaspoon vanilla
1 tablespoon water
1 tablespoon unsweetened
  cocoa powder

Sift flour, baking soda and salt in a bowl. In a separate bowl, beat butter 2 minutes until creamy. Add sugar and beat 3 minutes until fluffy. Add egg and vanilla. Add flour mixture to creamed mixture alternating with buttermilk in three batches. Roll dough by tablespoon into balls. Place 2-inches apart onto parchment paper lined baking sheet. Bake at 350 degrees 10 minutes until bottoms are golden browned. Cool on wire racks. Whisk together powdered sugar, syrup, juice, vanilla and water until smooth. Mix to desired consistency thicker than honey. Transfer half icing to a small bowl. Stir in cocoa. Thin with water if necessary. Spread white icing on half of each cookie's flat side and cocoa icing on the other half. Let stand 30 minutes.

Yield: 4 dozen cookies

A New York deli tradition and a childhood favorite of Nancy's husband Tim.

Old-Fashion Spritz

1½ cups butter
1 cup sugar
1 egg
1 teaspoon vanilla

½ teaspoon almond extract
4 cups all-purpose flour
1 teaspoon baking powder

Cream butter and sugar. Add egg, vanilla and almond extract. Beat well. Sift flour and baking powder and gradually add to creamed mixture. Mix to form smooth dough. Do not chill. On an ungreased cookie sheet, press dough through a cookie press into desired shapes. Decorate with sprinkles, colored sugar and maraschino cherry pieces. Bake at 400 degrees 8 minutes.

In Love with Chocolate Cookies

COOKIES
1½ sticks unsalted butter
¾ cup sugar
1 large egg yolk
1 teaspoon vanilla

1⅔ cups all-purpose flour
⅓ cup unsweetened cocoa powder
½ teaspoon salt

Beat the butter until light and fluffy. Add sugar and beat well. Beat in egg yolk, vanilla, flour, cocoa and salt. Form dough into a ball and pat into a disc. Roll out dough to ¼-inch thickness. Cut out cookies using a 2-inch heart shaped cookie cutter. Place on ungreased cookie sheets. Bake at 350 degrees 12 to 15 minutes. Transfer to rack and cool completely.

CHOCOLATE ICING
2 cups powdered sugar
6 tablespoons unsweetened
    cocoa powder

¼ cup milk

In a medium bowl, combine sugar, cocoa and milk. Stir until smooth and creamy. Spread a little icing over each cookie. Let harden 15 to 20 minutes.

Candy Cane Cookies

1½ sticks butter, softened	2 cups all-purpose flour
¾ cup sugar	½ teaspoon salt
1 egg	¼ teaspoon baking powder
½ teaspoon vanilla	1 teaspoon red food coloring
½ teaspoon peppermint extract	

Cream butter and sugar. Beat in egg, vanilla and peppermint extract. Combine flour, salt and baking powder. Stir into creamed mixture. Divide dough in half. Blend food coloring into one portion of the dough. Cover and refrigerate dough 30 minutes. Divide each dough mixture into thirty balls. Keep half dough chilled until ready to use. Roll each ball into a 5-inch rope. For each cane, pinch together one end of the red rope and one end of a white rope. Twist ropes together. Pinch together remaining ends. Place on a baking sheet and curve to form a cane. Repeat with remaining balls. Bake at 375 degrees 10 minutes. Do not allow to brown.

Yield: 30 cookies

Cardamom Butter Cookies

2 sticks butter, softened	½ teaspoon salt
1¼ cups sugar	1 teaspoon ground cardamom
2 eggs	½ teaspoon cinnamon
1 teaspoon vanilla	¼ teaspoon ground allspice
3 cups sifted all-purpose flour	
1 teaspoon baking powder	

Cream butter and sugar until light and fluffy. Add eggs and vanilla. Mix well. Sift together flour, baking powder, salt, cardamom, cinnamon and allspice. Stir into creamed mixture. Refrigerate dough. Roll out dough and cut with cutters. May also shape dough into a roll, chill and slice. Bake at 350 degrees 10 to 12 minutes, depending on thickness of cookies.

Yield: 7 dozen thin cookies

Chocolate Chip Pudding Cookies

3⅓ cups all-purpose flour
1½ teaspoons baking soda
3 sticks butter, softened
1 cup packed brown sugar
½ cup sugar

1 (6-ounce) package vanilla flavored
  instant pudding mix
1½ teaspoons vanilla
3 eggs
3 cups semi-sweet chocolate chips
½ cup chopped nuts (optional)

Combine flour and baking soda. Set aside. Cream butter, brown sugar, sugar, pudding mix and vanilla. Beat until smooth. Beat in eggs. Gradually add flour mixture. Stir in chocolate chips and nuts. Drop by teaspoonfuls onto baking sheet. Bake at 375 degrees 8 to 10 minutes.

Yield: 10 dozen cookies

This recipe came from one of Kathy's student's great grandmother. It was brought into the classroom and enjoyed by all of the children and adults.

Chocolate Kringles

1½ cups sugar
½ cup vegetable oil
3 (1-ounce) squares unsweetened
  chocolate, melted and cooled
2 teaspoons vanilla

3 eggs
¼ cup milk
2 cups all-purpose flour
2 teaspoons baking powder
Sifted powdered sugar

Combine sugar, oil, chocolate and vanilla. Add eggs, one at a time, beating well after each addition. Stir in milk. Combine flour and baking powder. Add to chocolate mixture. Refrigerate. Shape 1 tablespoon dough into balls. Roll in powdered sugar. Bake at 375 degrees 10 to 12 minutes. Dust with powdered sugar.

Yield: 4 dozen cookies

Cinnamon Stars

1 cup all-purpose flour
1½ teaspoons cinnamon
Pinch of salt
1 stick unsalted butter, softened

½ cup packed light brown sugar
1 large egg yolk
2 tablespoons sugar

Sift together flour, cinnamon and salt. Cream butter and brown sugar until light and fluffy. Beat in egg yolk until light. Add flour mixture and blend well. Cover and refrigerate at least 1 hour or overnight. Divide dough in half. Roll out half dough on a floured surface to ⅛-inch thickness. Cut dough with star shaped cutter. Place 2-inches apart on a lightly greased baking sheet. Roll out second half and cut with cookie cutter. Sprinkle cookies with sugar. Bake at 350 degrees 7 to 8 minutes or until edges begin to brown. Cool on a wire rack. Store in a tightly covered container.

Yield: 30 cookies

Ginger Snaps

1½ sticks butter, softened
2 cups sugar
2 eggs, well beaten
½ cup molasses
2 teaspoons vinegar
3¾ cups sifted all-purpose flour

1½ teaspoons baking soda
3 teaspoons ground ginger
½ teaspoon cinnamon
¼ teaspoon ground cloves
Sugar for rolling

Cream butter and sugar. Stir in eggs, molasses and vinegar. Sift together flour, baking soda, ginger, cinnamon and cloves. Add to creamed mixture and mix well. Shape dough into ¾-inch balls. Roll in sugar. Bake at 325 degrees 12 minutes.

Yield: 4 dozen cookies

We always roll the dough in pearl sugar.

Chocolate Peppermint Heart Cookies

1 stick butter, softened
⅔ cup sugar
1 egg
½ teaspoon vanilla
1 teaspoon peppermint extract
1¼ cups all-purpose flour

1 teaspoon baking powder
¼ teaspoon salt
Red food coloring
1 (8-ounce) package semi-sweet
  chocolate baking squares,
  melted

Beat butter and sugar until light and fluffy. Beat in egg, vanilla and peppermint extract. Combine flour, baking powder and salt. Beat into creamed mixture. Add a few drops food coloring until dough turns pink. Cover and refrigerate 1 hour. Roll out dough to ⅛-inch thickness on a lightly floured surface. Cut dough with 2-inch heart shaped cutter. Place 2-inches apart on parchment paper lined baking sheet. Refrigerate 30 minutes. Bake at 350 degrees 8 to 9 minutes until edges are lightly browned. Cool. Dip one side of each cookie in chocolate. Place on parchment paper. Let stand until chocolate is set. For an additional touch sprinkle with white nonpareils.

Yield: 5 dozen cookies

"Love in your heart
Wasn't put there to stay—
Love isn't love
'Til you give it away."

~ Oscar Hammerstein II, The Sound of Music

227

Italian Pizzelles

3 eggs
¾ cup sugar
1 stick butter, melted and cooled
1 teaspoon vanilla

1½ teaspoons anise extract
1¾ cups all-purpose flour
2 teaspoons baking powder

Beat eggs and sugar. Stir in butter, vanilla and anise. Sift together flour and baking powder. Stir into egg mixture. May refrigerate at this time. Drop by teaspoonfuls onto pizzelle maker. Cover lid for 30 seconds. Remove and cool on wire rack.

Yield: 30 pizzelles

We usually double this recipe. They are so thin, crisp and a hit with our family and friends. Often times we swirl in food coloring depending on the season or event. For a variation called Pizzelle con Ciccolate, add 3 tablespoons cocoa and 3 more tablespoons sugar to the above recipe.

Molasses Cookies

1 cup sugar
1½ sticks butter, softened
1 egg
¼ cup molasses
2 cups all-purpose flour
1½ teaspoons baking soda

½ teaspoon salt
1 teaspoon cinnamon
1 teaspoon ground ginger
½ teaspoon ground cloves
Sugar for rolling

Cream sugar and butter until fluffy. Add egg. Sift together flour, baking soda, salt, cinnamon, ginger and cloves. Stir into creamed mixture. Roll dough into balls the size of walnuts. Roll balls in sugar. Place on a greased baking sheet. Bake at 350 degrees 10 minutes.

Yield: 4 dozen cookies

Lemon-Butter Easter Egg Cookies with Royal Icing

DOUGH

1¾ cups sifted all-purpose flour	½ cup sugar
½ teaspoon baking powder	1 egg
¼ teaspoon salt	1 teaspoon lemon juice
1⅓ sticks unsalted butter, softened	2 tablespoons lemon zest

Sift together flour, baking powder and salt. Cream butter and sugar until light and fluffy. Beat in egg, juice and zest. Add flour mixture in three batches, stirring each time until dough is smooth. Roll dough on a floured surface to ⅛-inch thickness. Cut dough with an egg shaped cutter. Bake at 400 degrees 6 to 8 minutes or until lightly browned on bottom. Cool 5 minutes on baking sheet. Cool completely on racks.

ROYAL ICING

2 egg whites	1 teaspoon water (optional)
4 cups powdered sugar	Food coloring of choice

Beat egg whites and sugar 10 minutes until stiff. If too stiff, add water and beat. If too thin, continue beating or add ¼ cup powdered sugar. If desired, divide icing to make several colors. Add food coloring to icing and mix well. Spread icing over cookies.

Yield: 3 dozen cookies

To hang the Easter Egg Cookies on an Easter tree, make a ¼-inch diameter hole in the cookie using a skewer just before baking.

Orange Cookies

2 sticks butter, softened
½ cup sugar
½ cup packed brown sugar
1 egg, beaten
½ teaspoon baking soda

½ teaspoon salt
2 cups all-purpose flour
3 tablespoons orange juice
Zest of 1 orange
½ cup nuts

Cream butter, sugar and brown sugar until fluffy. Add egg. Sift together baking soda, salt and flour. Add flour mixture alternately with juice to creamed mixture. Stir in zest and nuts. Drop by teaspoonfuls onto a greased baking sheet. Bake at 375 degrees 8 to 10 minutes.

Yield: 4 dozen cookies

Savannah Chocolate Chews

2 cups chopped pecans
2¼ cups powdered sugar
¼ cup plus 2 tablespoons
   unsweetened cocoa powder
2 tablespoons all-purpose flour

¼ teaspoon salt
3 large egg whites
¾ teaspoon vanilla
1 (1-ounce) semi-sweet chocolate
   baking square, grated

Spread pecans on a baking sheet. Toast at 325 degrees 7 to 9 minutes, stirring occasionally until lightly browned. Cool in a bowl. Combine powdered sugar, cocoa powder, flour and salt. Beat in egg whites, one at a time, until blended. Add vanilla and beat 1½ minutes. Fold in pecans and chocolate. Drop dough by heaping tablespoonfuls about 2-inches apart onto parchment lined baking sheets. Bake at 325 degrees 15 to 18 minutes until edges are browned and centers are soft. Slide the cookies still attached to parchment paper to wire racks. Cool completely and peel off parchment.

Yield: 24 cookies

This recipe comes from Gottlieb's Bakery in Savannah, Georgia. The bakery opened in 1884 and unfortunately went out of business in the 1990's. It continues to be a favorite of the old south!

Oatmeal Raisin Cookies

1 (6-ounce) package raisins
3 cups dry quick oats
2 cups all-purpose flour
1 teaspoon cinnamon
½ teaspoon baking powder
½ teaspoon baking soda
½ teaspoon salt
1⅓ sticks butter, softened

½ cup vegetable shortening
1 cup packed light brown sugar
1 cup sugar
2 large eggs
1 teaspoon vanilla
½ cup chopped walnuts
or pecans

Place raisins in a bowl. Cover with hot water. Set aside. Combine oats, flour, cinnamon, baking powder, baking soda and salt. In another bowl, beat butter and shortening until light and fluffy. Add brown sugar and sugar and beat until smooth. Beat in eggs and vanilla. Stir in all but 1 cup oats mixture until evenly mixed. Drain raisins. Mix reserved oat mixture, raisins and nuts. Fold into dough and mix well. Shape dough into golf ball size balls with lightly greased hands. Place 2-inches apart on a baking sheet and flatten down the top. Bake at 375 degrees 8 to 11 minutes or until lightly browned but soft in the center. Do not over bake. Place baking sheet on a wire rack, cool cookies 1 to 2 minutes. Transfer cookies to racks to cool completely.

Yield: 30 cookies

Peach Blossoms

1½ sticks butter, softened
1 (3-ounce) package cream cheese, softened
¾ cup sugar

1 tablespoon lemon zest
2 cups all-purpose flour
¼ teaspoon salt
¼ cup peach preserves

Beat butter, cream cheese, sugar and zest until light and fluffy. On low speed, beat in flour and salt. Flatten dough in a disc and wrap in plastic wrap. Refrigerate 30 minutes. Roll dough into small balls. Press a well into the center. Fill with preserves. Bake at 350 degrees 10 to 12 minutes.

Yield: 3 dozen cookies

Snappy Macaroons

1 (14-ounce) package shredded
   coconut
1 (14-ounce) can sweetened
   condensed milk

1 teaspoon vanilla
1 (10-ounce) jar red or green
   maraschino cherries, stems
   removed and halved

Combine coconut and milk. Add vanilla. Drop batter by teaspoonfuls onto a parchment lined baking sheet. Place a cherry half in the center of each cookie. Bake at 350 degrees 10 to 12 minutes. Immediately remove from baking sheet. Cool on a rack. Carefully place on a dish. May need to gently reshape cookie.

Yield: 30 cookies

Sweetheart Cookies

4 cups all-purpose flour
½ teaspoon salt
1 teaspoon baking powder
2 sticks butter, softened
2 cups sugar
2 eggs

¼ cup blackberry brandy
1 teaspoon vanilla
1 (12-ounce) jar seedless red
   raspberry preserves
Powdered sugar

Sift together flour, salt and baking powder. Beat butter and sugar until fluffy. Add eggs, brandy and vanilla. Mix well. Gradually add flour mixture. Mix until well blended. Wrap dough and refrigerate at least 30 minutes. Roll one-third of dough on a floured surface to ⅛-inch thickness. Cut dough with 2 to 3-inch heart shaped cutter. Place on parchment lined baking sheet. Bake at 400 degrees 4 to 5 minutes. Do not allow to brown. Cool on wire racks. To assemble, spread ¼ to ½ teaspoon preserves on one cookie and top with another to form a sandwich. Dust with powdered sugar.

Yield: 4 dozen sandwich cookies

Strawberry Cookies

DOUGH

4 sticks butter, softened
1 cup powdered sugar
2 tablespoons red food coloring
1 tablespoon vanilla

4¼ cups all-purpose flour
1 teaspoon salt
2 cups dry quick oats

Beat butter until creamy. Gradually beat in powdered sugar until smooth. Stir in food coloring and vanilla. Combine flour and salt. Add to creamed mixture, blending well. Stir in oats. Shape dough to look like strawberries. Place wide end down (top of strawberry) on a greased baking sheet. Bake at 325 degrees 25 minutes or until firm to touch.

FROSTING

1⅓ cups sugar
¼ cup water
⅛ teaspoon cream of tartar
2 egg whites

2 teaspoons green food coloring
1 teaspoon vanilla
Pinch of salt

Combine sugar, water and cream of tartar in a saucepan. Bring to boil. Reduce heat and cook to thread stage (230 degrees on a candy thermometer) or until syrup spins a 2-inch thread when dropped from a spoon. Beat egg whites to a soft peak. Pour a stream of hot syrup into egg whites, while beating. Add all the syrup and beat until frosting is very thick and forms soft peaks. Stir in food coloring, vanilla and salt. While frosting is warm, dip in the top of each cookie. Place on rack to dry.

Yield: 7 dozen cookies

Wall Street Kisses

2 sticks unsalted butter, softened
½ cup powdered sugar plus more
    for dusting
1 teaspoon vanilla

2 cups all-purpose flour
1 cup finely chopped walnuts
1 (6-ounce) package milk chocolate
    kisses

Beat butter, powdered sugar and vanilla until light and fluffy. Add flour and walnuts. Beat on low speed until blended. Shape dough around kiss, forming a sphere. Bake at 375 degrees 12 minutes or until set. Dust with powdered sugar. Cool on wire rack.

Yield: 3 dozen cookies

Baseball Bars

DOUGH

1½ sticks butter
1 cup packed brown sugar
¼ cup light corn syrup

¼ cup chunky peanut butter
1 teaspoon vanilla
4 cups dry quick oats

Melt butter, brown sugar and syrup in a saucepan. Mix well. Add peanut butter and vanilla. Mix until smooth. Stir in oats. Press mixture into a greased 9 x 9 x 2-inch baking dish. Bake at 375 degrees 15 minutes.

TOPPING

1 (12-ounce) package semi-sweet
    chocolate chips
1 (12-ounce) package butterscotch
    chips

⅔ cup chunky peanut butter
1 cup chopped nuts

Combine chocolate chips, butterscotch chips, peanut butter and nuts in a saucepan. Cook and stir over medium heat until smooth. Spread over cooked bars. Cool and cut into squares.

Yield: 16 to 20 bars

Butterscotch Strips

2 sticks butter, softened
1 cup packed brown sugar
1 egg
2 cups all-purpose flour
1 teaspoon vanilla

2 eggs, beaten
½ cup packed brown sugar
1 cup sliced pecans
½ cup packed brown sugar

Cream butter and brown sugar until fluffy. Add egg, flour and vanilla and mix well. Divide batter in half and spread as thin as possible on two large baking sheets. Spread eggs over batter. Sprinkle each baking sheet with ¼ cup brown sugar and ½ cup nuts. Top with remaining sugar. Bake at 350 degrees 10 to 12 minutes. Cut into strips while hot. Cool in pan.

Yield: 3 to 4 dozen

Old-Fashioned Hermits

2 cups all-purpose flour
1 teaspoon baking soda
½ teaspoon salt
1 teaspoon cinnamon
½ teaspoon ground cloves
2 teaspoons ground ginger

¾ cup vegetable shortening
1 cup sugar
2 eggs, beaten
¼ cup molasses
1 cup raisins

Sift together flour, baking soda, salt, cinnamon, cloves and ginger. Set aside. Cream shortening and sugar. Add eggs, molasses and raisins. Blend in flour mixture. Refrigerate 2 to 3 hours. Place dough on a baking sheet and top with plastic wrap. Press dough flat over entire baking sheet. Bake at 350 degrees 10 to 12 minutes. Cool completely. Cut into bars.

Yield: 30 bars

Chocolate Covered Cherries

2 sticks butter
1 (14-ounce) can sweetened
    condensed milk
2 (16-ounce) packages plus 1 cup
    powdered sugar
1 teaspoon salt

1 (3½-ounce) can coconut
3 cups pecans, finely ground
4 (8-ounce) bottles maraschino
    cherries
2 pound dark chocolate baking bar,
    melted

Melt butter and allow cooling. Pour into a large bowl. Add milk, powdered sugar, salt, coconut and pecans. Mix until smooth and creamy. Shape batter into small balls. Wrap balls around cherries. Place on a wax paper lined baking sheet. Refrigerate until set. Gently dip cherries in chocolate and replace on wax paper to harden.

Yield: 120 cherries

Mommy's Peanut Butter Fudge

2 cups sugar
⅔ cup milk
1 (15-ounce) jar marshmallow
    creme

1 cup peanut butter
1 teaspoon vanilla

Combine sugar and milk in a saucepan. Cook to a softball stage. Remove from heat. In a warm mixing bowl, combine marshmallow creme, peanut butter and vanilla. Add cooked syrup and mix well. Pour into a buttered 8 x 8 x 2-inch baking dish.

Yield: 12 to 15 servings

Mommy made and served this at our old Thanksgiving gatherings.

This & That

"I don't know of anything in the entire world more wonderful to look at than a nest with eggs in it. An egg, because it contains life, is the most perfect thing there is. It is beautiful and mysterious."

~ TRUMPET OF THE SWAN

Cranberry Raspberry Sauce

1 (12-ounce) package cranberries
1 cup water
1½ cups sugar

1 (12-ounce) package frozen
  raspberries, thawed

Combine cranberries and water in a saucepan. Stir in sugar. Cook over medium heat 5 to 10 minutes until cranberries have almost popped Add raspberries and cook 5 minutes more. Stir until well blended. Serve warm or cold. Store in refrigerator up to 2 weeks.

Yield: 2½ cups

Serve with scones or as an accompaniment to turkey, chicken or pork. Kathy made it with cranberries, raspberries and blackberries. Our mother came up with the idea to serve it in small antique crystal bowls over a scoop of vanilla ice cream. It was a sight to behold and delicious too!

Simple Red Sauce

2 tablespoons olive oil
1 medium onion, diced
2 garlic cloves, minced
2 (28-ounce) cans crushed
  tomatoes

1½ teaspoons salt
½ teaspoon pepper
¼ teaspoon crushed red pepper
1 tablespoon dried basil
2 teaspoons dried oregano

Heat oil in a large skillet. Sauté onions until tender. Add garlic and cook 2 minutes. Add tomatoes, salt, pepper, red pepper, basil and oregano. Simmer 1 hour or more until thickened.

Yield: 6 to 8 servings

Hunters Sauce

½ cup packed brown sugar
½ cup ketchup
4 tablespoons butter
¼ cup apple jelly
1 teaspoon cinnamon

½ teaspoon ground allspice
½ teaspoon pepper
¼ teaspoon ground cloves
3 tablespoons lemon juice

Combine brown sugar, ketchup, butter, jelly, cinnamon, allspice, pepper, cloves and juice in a saucepan. Cover and simmer, stirring occasionally, until smooth.

Yield: 1⅓ cups

Kathy's sister-in-law, Lil, says that this sauce is great with lamb. Another special note about this recipe is that it came from the Middleburg, VA hunt country.

Tangy Barbecue Sauce

2 garlic cloves, minced
1 cup minced onion
4 tablespoons butter
1 cup ketchup
½ cup water
½ cup packed brown sugar

1 teaspoon salt
½ teaspoon cayenne pepper
2 teaspoons Worcestershire
   sauce
¼ cup molasses
¼ cup vinegar

Combine garlic, onions, butter, ketchup, water, brown sugar, salt, cayenne, Worcestershire sauce, molasses and vinegar in a saucepan. Simmer 30 minutes.

Yield: 2 cups

For a twist to the already dynamic flavor, add ¼ cup peach preserves. Delicious!

Cranberry, Cherry and Walnut Chutney

2 cups dried tart cherries
1 cup fresh cranberries
1 cup raisins
1 cup sugar
½ cup apple cider vinegar
½ cup finely chopped celery

6 tablespoons apple juice
½ teaspoon crushed red pepper
1 tablespoon lemon zest
1 cup toasted and coarsely
  chopped walnuts

Combine cherries, cranberries, raisins, sugar, vinegar, celery, juice, red pepper, zest and walnuts in a 2-quart saucepan. Cook over medium heat 20 minutes, stirring occasionally. Cool to room temperature. Cover tightly and refrigerate. Chutney thickens as it cools. Store in refrigerator up to 2 weeks.

Yield: 6 to 8 servings

Cranberry-Fig Relish

4 cups fresh cranberries
1 cup dried figs
2 tablespoons minced fresh mint
  leaves

1 cup orange marmalade
2 tablespoons balsamic vinegar

Chop cranberries and figs in a food processor until coarsely chopped. Transfer to a bowl. Stir in mint. Whisk together marmalade and vinegar. Add to cranberry mixture and stir well. Cover and refrigerate at least 2 hours or up to a week.

Yield: 4 cups

Southern Peach Chutney

2 cups peeled and diced peaches
½ cup minced yellow onion
4 teaspoons peeled and minced
   ginger

½ cup finely diced sweet red pepper
½ cup packed light brown sugar
½ cup sugar
2 tablespoons cider vinegar

Combine peaches, onions, ginger, red peppers, brown sugar, sugar and vinegar in a saucepan. Stir well. Bring to boil. Reduce heat and simmer 25 to 30 minutes until chutney thickens and is syrupy. Remove from heat and cool. Store in refrigerator for 2 weeks.

Yield: 3 cups

Great topper on grilled pork or on fried green tomatoes topped with sour cream.

Chow Chow

4 cups finely chopped zucchini and
   yellow squash
1½ cups finely chopped onion
¾ cup finely chopped sweet red
   pepper
¾ cup finely chopped bell pepper
4½ teaspoons pickling salt

¾ cup sugar
2 cups cider vinegar
1 teaspoon celery seeds
1 teaspoon mustard seeds
1 teaspoon dry mustard
1 teaspoon ground ginger
1 teaspoon turmeric

Combine zucchini, yellow squash, onions, pepper and salt in a large bowl. Cover and let stand 3 hours at room temperature. Drain excess liquid. Rinse and drain again. Transfer to a nonreactive stockpot. Stir in sugar, vinegar, celery seeds, mustard seeds, mustard, ginger and turmeric. Bring to boil. Reduce heat and simmer 20 minutes. Transfer to an airtight container. Cover and refrigerate at least 1 week. Store refrigerated for one month.

Yield: 8 to 10 servings

This relish is delicious with hamburgers and hot dogs.

Tim's Barbecue Sauce

1 (18-ounce) bottle Kraft original
   barbecue sauce

½ (12-ounce) can frozen orange
   juice concentrate, thawed
¼ cup dry red wine

Combine barbecue sauce, juice and wine. Stir until concentrate dissolves and is well blended. Use on chicken, London broil or pork.

Yield: 2 cups

Piccalilli

8 cups coarsely chopped zucchini
   and yellow squash
1 cup coarsely chopped mixture of
   sweet red and orange peppers
1 cup coarsely chopped celery
2 large onions, coarsely chopped
2 cups fresh corn kernels
⅓ cup pickling salt
1 cup sugar

½ cup packed light brown sugar
2 cups cider vinegar
1 tablespoon peeled and chopped
   ginger
1 teaspoon celery seed
1 teaspoon dry mustard
1 teaspoon crushed red pepper
1 teaspoon ground ginger
1 teaspoon turmeric

Combine zucchini, squash, peppers, celery, onions, corn and salt in a large bowl. Cover and let stand 3 hours at room temperature. Drain liquid. Rinse and drain again. Transfer to a nonreactive stockpot. Add sugar, brown sugar, vinegar, ginger, celery seed, mustard, red pepper, ginger and turmeric. Bring to boil, stirring constantly. Reduce heat and simmer 20 minutes. Transfer to a nonreactive container. Cover and refrigerate at least 1 week. Store refrigerated for one month.

Yield: 8 to 10 servings

Cranberry Mustard

¾ cup packed brown sugar
½ cup Dijon mustard

¾ cup cranberries, fresh or frozen
¼ cup molasses

Combine brown sugar, mustard, cranberries and molasses in a saucepan. Bring to boil. Reduce heat and cook 5 minutes, stirring constantly.

Yield: 1½ cups

This mustard is easy to make and tastes delicious on a turkey sandwich. You may also use it as a glaze on chicken or turkey!

Cranberry Butter

1 stick unsalted butter, softened
2 tablespoons powdered sugar
⅛ teaspoon orange zest

3 tablespoons chopped fresh cranberries

Combine butter and powdered sugar in a food processor or blender. Process until smooth. Add zest and cranberries. Process until just mixed. Press mixture into individual butter mold, cookie cutters or a ball. Serve cold or room temperature. May refrigerate for several days.

Yield: ¾ cup

This butter may be served with bread during your Thanksgiving meal. If using a cookie cutter, fill cutter and refrigerate until firm. The cookie cutter may be removed by carefully pushing the butter out onto a plate or butter dish.

Autumn Spice Butter

1 stick butter, softened
1 teaspoon honey

½ teaspoon pumpkin pie spice

Blend together butter, honey and pie spice. Press mixture into butter molds or cookie cutter shapes. Refrigerate. Remove butter from mold before serving.

Yield: ½ cup

Strawberry Butter

1 (8-ounce) package cream cheese, softened
1 stick unsalted butter, softened

½-¾ cup powdered sugar
1 teaspoon vanilla
8 large fresh strawberries, mashed

Beat cream cheese, butter and powdered sugar until light and fluffy. Add vanilla and strawberries. Beat until well blended. Serve with croissants or scones.

Yield: 1½ cups

"Kick On" Spices

2½ tablespoons paprika
2 tablespoons onion salt
2 tablespoons garlic powder
2½ teaspoons pepper
1 tablespoon cayenne pepper

1 tablespoon dried oregano
1 tablespoon dried thyme
½ teaspoon dried lemon zest
½ teaspoon ground chipotle pepper

Combine paprika, onion salt, garlic powder, pepper, cayenne pepper, oregano, thyme, zest and chipotle pepper. Mix well. Store in an airtight container. Great for marinades and seasonings.

Yield: ⅔ cup

Cardamom Toast

2 tablespoons sugar
½ teaspoon ground cardamom

4 slices firm white bread
Unsalted butter, softened

Combine sugar and cardamom. Mix well. Toast bread slices on both sides. Butter toast on both sides. Cut each slice into 4 triangles, trimming off crust. Gently press into cardamom mixture, coating on both sides. Arrange on a platter and serve warm.

Yield: 16 toast triangles

Great with afternoon tea!

Tourshi

4 carrots, peeled and quartered
1 small head cauliflower, separated
    into florets
4 stalks celery, cut into 4-inch
    pieces
2 garlic cloves, peeled

4 sprigs fresh dill
1 quart water
1 cup cider vinegar
¼ cup salt
1 tablespoon sugar

Cut carrots into 4-inch pieces. Sterilize 2-quart jars in boiling water. Pack jars with carrots, cauliflower and celery. Add one garlic and two dill sprigs to each jar. Pack jars tightly. Place ring around jar. Combine water, vinegar, salt and sugar in a saucepan. Bring to boil. Pour enough hot brine into jars to overflow. Seal lids as tightly as possible. Let stand 2 to 4 weeks depending on how tart you like them. The longer you leave them, the more tart they will become.

Yield: 8 servings

Our Armenian grandmother made these all the time. They were a tradition at our large family Thanksgiving gatherings at Grandma's house.

Toasted Spiced Pecans

1 tablespoon unsalted butter   ⅛ teaspoon cayenne pepper
1 cup pecan halves   ¼ teaspoon salt

Melt butter in a saucepan. Stir in pecans, cayenne and salt. Cook and stir 1 minute, being careful not to burn. Spread pecans on a baking sheet. Bake at 350 degrees 4 minutes. They should be shiny with a lightly toasted aroma, color and flavor. Remove from oven and place on paper towels to absorb oil. Cool to room temperature. Store in an airtight container.

Yield: 1 cup

A great little snack with your 5 o'clock cocktail!

Jemima's Chocolate Nests

3 tablespoons butter   7 rounded tablespoons rice cereal
2 tablespoons corn syrup   12 paper cupcake liners
4 tablespoons cocoa powder   Jelly beans
7 rounded tablespoons cornflakes

Melt butter and syrup in a saucepan. Whisk in cocoa until smooth. Add cornflakes and rice cereal. Mix until well coated. Drop mixture by spoonfuls into cupcake liners. To form the nests, press a well in the middle of each nest with your thumb. Refrigerate until set. Place a few jelly beans in each.

Yield: 12 nests

Jemima's nests can be set at place settings for spring luncheons or dinners.

Spring Chocolate Nests

1 (14-ounce) can sweetened
condensed milk
2 cups semi sweet chocolate chips

2 (5-ounce) cans thin chow mein
noodles

Line 2 baking sheets with foil and lightly coat with cooking spray. Scrape milk into a saucepan. Add chocolate chips. Cook and stir until blended and smooth. Place noodles in a bowl. Pour chocolate sauce over noodles. Stir until coated. Drop generous ½ cupfuls onto prepared sheets. Lightly spray fingertips with cooking spray. Press a well into nests making a depression in the center to hold candies. Refrigerate 30 minutes or until set. Peel off foil. Fill with candies or Jordan almonds.

Yield: 8 to 10 nests

Edible Springtime Nests

1 stick butter
1 (10-ounce) package large
marshamllows

12 shredded wheat biscuits,
crumbled

Melt butter in a large saucepan over low heat. Add marshmallows and stir until melted. Remove from heat and stir in shredded wheat. Cool mixture slightly. Place 1 tablespoon warm mixture on a wax paper. Shape mixture into a bird nest. Cool completely. Fill with speckled chocolate eggs.

Yield: 20 nests

Old-Fashioned Butter Cream Frosting

6 tablespoons butter, softened
1 (16-ounce) package powdered
   sugar, sifted

¼ cup half-and-half
1½ teaspoons vanilla

Cream butter with half powdered sugar. Blend well. Beat in 2 tablespoons half-and-half and vanilla. Gradually blend in remaining powdered sugar. Add enough half-and-half to reach spreading consistency.

Yield: Frosting for two 8 or 9-inch cake layers

Rhubarb Sauce

3 cups rhubarb, cut into
   1-inch pieces
½-¾ cup sugar

¼ cup water
½ teaspoon cinnamon

Combine rhubarb, sugar, water and cinnamon in a saucepan. Bring to boil. Cover and simmer 5 minutes until tender.

Yield: 2 cups

Here is an old-fashioned recipe that is loved by all. Spoon over vanilla ice cream or angel food cake.

Crème Fraîche

1 cup heavy cream
¼ cup buttermilk

1 tablespoon lemon juice

Blend cream, buttermilk and juice. Cover and let stand at room temperature 6 to 8 hours. Refrigerate until ready to use.

Yield: 1¼ cups

Index

Cranberry and Dried Fruit Relish 74
Cranberry Applesauce 77
Cranberry Brownies 214
Cranberry Harvest Chicken 113
Cranberry Pecan Spread 21
Cranberry Salad Ring 61
Cranberry Salsa with Brie 25
Cranberry Turkey Salad 48
Cranberry Upside-Down Muffins 150
Diamond, Ruby, Emerald and Sapphire Scones. . . 164
Star Spangled Muffins. 159

CUCUMBERS
Armenian Cucumber Salad. 56
Cucumber Boats. 18
Cucumber Dill Dip. 25
Tomato, Watermelon and Cucumber Salad. 63

DATES
Date Nut Pumpkin Pie 199
Date Pudding. 212
Mom's Dark Date Nut Bread 160
Stuffed Dates 21

DESSERTS
Brownies and Bars
Baseball Bars. 234
Blondes Have More Fun Toffee Blondies 213
Butterscotch Strips 235
Childhood Devil Dogs. 219
Cranberry Brownies 214
Gentlemen Prefer Blondies 213
George Washington's Cherry Brownies 215
Gold Brick Brownies 214
Hoist the Flag Brownies 217
Old-Fashioned Hermits 235
Palm Beach Citrus Brownies 216
Raspberry Crumb Bars 218
Cakes
Banana Ice Box Cake. 179
Black Tie Cheesecake 174
Blueberry Cake with Crumb Topping 204
Blueberry Coffee Cake 205
Bourbon Brown Sugar Pound Cake. 189
Chocolate Sour Cream Pound Cake 190
Cousin Robin's Gingerbread Cake 183
Daffodil Cake 182
Everglades Coconut Layer Cake 181
Gingerbread with Lemon Orange Glaze 207
Hotel Del Milky Way Layer Cake 177
Hot Fudge Sundae Cake 176
Kentucky Glazed Orange Cake 184
Maine Blueberry Gingerbread 202
Maple Pudding Cake. 210
Old-Fashioned Blueberry Cake 187
Perfect Pound Cake. 191
Peter Rabbit's Carrot Cake. 180
Pineapple Upside Down Cake. 185
Popcorn Cake 183
Pumpkin Cake 186
Rhubarb Cake 188

Santa Baby Chocolate Cake. 175
Simple Devil's Food Cake 176
Swedish Almond Coffee Cake 205
Wartime Chocolate Cake. 178
Zucchini Cake. 178
Candy
Chocolate Covered Cherries 236
Mommy's Peanut Butter Fudge 236
Cobblers
Fruit Cobblers. 201
Peach Cobbler. 201
Rhubarb Cobbler 201
Savannah Peach Cobbler. 200
Summer Blackberry Crisp 202
Cookies
Black and White Cookies 222
Candy Cane Cookies. 224
Cardamom Butter Cookies 224
Chocolate Chip Pudding Cookies 225
Chocolate Kringles 225
Chocolate Peppermint Heart Cookies 227
Cinnamon Stars 226
Ginger Snaps 226
In Love with Chocolate Cookies 223
Italian Pizzelles 228
Lemon-Butter Easter Egg Cookies
    with Royal Icing 229
Molasses Cookies 228
Oatmeal Raisin Cookies 231
Old-Fashion Spritz 223
Orange Cookies 230
Peach Blossoms. 231
Pizzelle con Ciccolate 228
Savannah Chocolate Chews 230
Snappy Macaroons 232
Strawberry Cookies. 233
Sweetheart Cookies. 232
Wall Street Kisses 234
Frostings, Icings and Glazes
Chocolate Cream Cheese Frosting. 179
Chocolate Icing. 223
Cream Cheese Frosting 179, 186
Creamy Glaze 182
Lemon Curd and Cream Cheese
    Filling and Frosting. 180
Lemon Glaze. 182
Royal Icing 229
Seven Minute Frosting 181
Pies
Apple-Ginger Cranberry Pie 190
Apple Pie 193
Banbury Turnovers 200
Blue-Barb Pie 192
Blueberry Pie 195
Buttermilk Crust. 196
Buttermilk Pie 193
Cousin Catherine's Cranberry Pie 194
Custard Pecan Pie 198
Date Nut Pumpkin Pie 199

Index